Own Your Story

Own Your Story

Take Off The Mask and Be Your Authentic Self

Shellinda Miller

Scriptures marked NIV are taken from the NEW INTERNATIONAL VERSION (NIV): Scripture is taken from The Holy Bible: New International Version®, NIV®, Copyright© 1973, 1978, 1984, 2011 by Biblica, Inc ™. Used by permission. All rights reserved worldwide.

Scriptures marked KJV are taken from the King James Version (KJV): Scripture taken from the New King James Version. Copyright © 1982 by Thomas Nelson, Inc. Used by permission. All rights reserved.

https://www.cmgww.com/sports/ashe/biography/

https://www.higherperspectives.com

ISBN: 978-0-578-53511-1

This book is dedicated to

Sara Alice Harris Barton
Mother of my mother
Carolyn Elaine Barton Sexton

Augusta Sease Hill
Mother of my father
Donald Rae Hill

I could never thank you enough for making it possible for my being here. Your unconditional love has never gone unnoticed. I now know, understand, and appreciate the value of sitting in absolute quietness. Thank you both for teaching how to be still. The things I have learned and times I heard from God when there was no talking, no television, and no sound. I miss your company. Thank you for everything you've taught me without words but by your grace and your actions. I am forever grateful that God chose you to birth my mother and my father. You are loved and you are missed. Forever in heart...... Pershing and Front.

Table of Contents

FORWARD

By Carolyn E. Sexton

It was a great honor to be asked by Shellinda, to write a foreword to her amazing book. I have known Shellinda all of her life, after all, I am the one who birthed her. When she told me was going to write a book and what is was going to be about, I knew that she would do a good job, not only because she is my daughter but because I share her values and beliefs and I believe deeply in living life authentically. Writing and sharing these details wasn't the easiest thing in the world for Shellinda, but she has a passion for people and a tremendous gift to serve others and that's what dictates her writing this book. That coupled with the fact that she has always had a terrific gift of storytelling and connecting with other people. She wrote this book not only to tell her own story but to also share how we can all live mask free and live our lives authentically.

In this book, Shellinda is blunt about her struggles, her failures, and successes. She walks you through the tests, trials, losses, and wins in a very clear way, with lots of advice based on her experiences. She begins immediately with a terrifying period in her life, a period that I can identify with. Shellinda isn't alone, not by a long shot, I too believe we all have worn a mask or two or three or four.

What makes this book most significant to me is the way she uses what she's learned, often the hard way, to help the rest of us recognize the masks we wear can come off and most importantly, help us understand the importance of being authentic so we can live a healthy freer life. I believe this book has great value to all people, especially women.

For thirty years of my daughter's life and military career, she has lead hundreds and thousands of men and women, and their families, in the United States Navy. As much as she has poured into the lives of others, she always keeps her priority of taking care of her home, her family first. Being a leader and a mother at home starts with us being positive role models for our children.

Ultimately, I encourage you to use this book to help awaken yourself, to discover who you are, to be vulnerable and all the possibilities you're holding to be who you were called to be.

Acknowledgement

Finally, brethren, whatsoever things are true, whatsoever things are honest, whatsoever things are just, whatsoever things are pure, whatsoever things are lovely, whatsoever things are of good report; if there be any virtue, and if there be any praise, think on these things. (Phil 4:8 KJV)

For my mom, affectionately known as "Nan", thank you for your wisdom. You are the heart and soul, the rock of our family, I could not have asked for a better example when it comes to parenting, love, loyalty, support, compassion and grace. Your heart is so big and your love for family, community and others is genuine and constant. You are tough and resourceful, devoted and loving, and you always believed in me, even when you disapproved of my choices. You gave me and my siblings the best childhood, I would change anything about the way or where were raised. I learned life's most valuable lessons from you and for that I'm forever grateful and blessed to call you mom. Thank you for placing me in a leadership environment from my earliest recollection.

For my father, the first man I loved. I am forever thankful to the Lord Almighty for the 34 years I had with you. Your unconditional love taught me so much at such an early age. Thank you for keeping my siblings and I close to one another. I miss our talks, our laughs and the way you would end every conversation, "okay, you okay?" followed by "I love you." I miss you daddy.

For Cavon and Casuan, my first and second heartbeat. I am the biggest fan of your lives. You are amazing gifts from God and words could never express the depth of my love for you. From day one it has been an honor to be your mother and I live in gratitude because of your existence. Because of you I have learned that loving includes laughing right through the washing machine, the crash, and missteps. You have made me stronger, better and more fulfilled than I could have ever imagined. With humor and love, you supported me with this project and helped me accurately describe my thoughts on paper. Thank you for the tidbits of motivation and honest feedback along the way. I love you to the moon and back and you will forever be my sunshine. May God continue to birth all the greatness that He has placed within you. I look forward to sharing the journey of your storytelling. Keep your eyes on Him.

For my husband Okkerse, the CEO and CFO for our family. You are truly the gift that keeps on giving. You have given me an unbelievable gift of love and unconditional support in all that I desire and set out to accomplishment. Thank you for helping me find my sweet spot and staying the course when things got tough and celebrating my successes and my setbacks. I cannot thank you enough for everything you have done in supporting me with this project. You graciously gave an extra set of eyes and helped me describe the story inside my head. Daily you provided keen insight and honest feedback. You allowed me to focus on this project and pushed me when necessary. Thank you for sharing with me in the belief that God is first and foremost in our lives and with Him all things are possible.

For I know the plans I have for you," declares the Lord, "plans to prosper you and not to harm you, plans to give you hope and a future. (Jer 29:11 NIV)

Special Thanks:

To Victoria and Ashley Barnes; my daughters from another mother. It has been a blessing to have you as part of our family for the past 11 years, it is God purposed and God ordained A special note of gratitude for your editorial work and giving my book a final wash. You both have provided keen insight, honest feedback and ongoing support with this project. We are all so thankful and blessed to have you in our lives. I love you forever.

Telling your story is a surreal process. I am forever indebted to Jasmine Womack, CEO and Senior Director of P31 Publishing Company, for your guidance, keen insight, and ongoing support and encouragement in sharing my story.

Introduction

No one had any idea that something was going on in my life, something major. The very idea of anyone knowing overwhelmed me, it seemed easy just to keep things quiet. For seven months I have kept this change in my life hidden from everyone at work. I work five days a week, and every four days staying overnight onboard the ship for duty. If anyone found out this secret I was carrying, my life would immediately change and that was enough to convince me that silence was the best option. But it wasn't easy. I was already feeling stressed. Keeping this secret was adding a heavy dose of guilt, shame, and fear was asking for a depressing time. So, I said nothing. Then one April morning the mask I had so secretly had been wearing was literally ripped from me and the day I knew was going to come, was here. I went into labor a month early. He was here, my son was born, healthy and alive.

When I talk about the mask, I am talking about the invisible protective shields we use to hide behind to protect ourselves from our pain, fears, shame, embarrassment, our past, or particular personalities we choose to project to others while hiding our authentic self.

Follow me as I share my journey towards authentic living, which began when I learned to embrace and come to terms with my weaknesses and discovered the different masks I wore.

Since taking off my masks I've learned about the many other reasons we choose to conceal our real selves from those around us. I've also spent time exploring the ways in which I believe God encourages us to remove our masks and the tools he gives us to keep living mask free.

It is my desire that sharing my story will help you find the courage to be yourself and discover your authenticity. My prayer is that this book will help each of you as you journey through your own life, traveling on the way to greater authenticity.

Some people may not be aware of the mask they wear or the reasons why they wear them. It is my desire to help you discover your authenticity as you read further. I pray that God will reveal to you the times you are wearing a mask or the things you are concealing and teach you how-to walk-in victory as you learn to live authentically.

In not sharing this, I was hiding my true self, the me I love and value. I am learning and growing every day with an attitude of gratitude. I am always working at being the best me I can be as I live my truth.

PART I:

Reactivate Your Authenticity: Acceptance And Shifting

CHAPTER 1

❖❖❖

No One Is Exempt

> *"Behind every mask there is a face, and behind that a story."*
> *— Marty Rubin*

A few things I have learned is that we only know what people tell us and sometimes what they show us. We make assumptions and have opinions but knowing something for certain, is totally different. I can remember this applying to me. How would anyone know that I experienced physical abuse at the hands of a boyfriend, multiple times, well before my 18th birthday, except if I tell them, or they witness the events? How would one know I hid a pregnancy while onboard a ship for nine months unless I told them? How would anyone know I was going through a divorce or a major professional transition unless I told them?

Those things are a part of my life experiences, my story, that I masked very well. I am a perfect example of "you only know what people tell you or sometimes what they show you."

When you think of a mask what image comes to your mind? What do you see? Glitz, glitter, bright colors, rhinestones, or a dark frightening image? I'm not talking about the plastic Halloween masks we wore as kids, with the thin elastic string that went behind our heads to secure the mask in place. Most masks have a story, they present an image of something or someone we want to try to become, even if it's just for a moment. The masks I'm talking about are the invisible masks that we don from day to day that represent our "pretend self ", or the roles we play in our lives, the mask we put on to conceal or hide some part of our true being.

Before I formed you in the womb I knew you, before you were born I set you apart. Jeremiah 1:5 (NIV)

We have all worn a mask of one kind or another, no one is exempt. The reason we wear masks vary and are probably different for each of us. Our masks change based on the situation or circumstance.

We wear a mask to hide the things we're going through that we may not want others to see or know, to cover our flaws, fears, shame, pain, secrets, financial hardships, and emotional struggles. Sometimes we wear a mask to be something or someone we're not and for a ton of other reasons. Regardless of the reason we all wear or have worn a mask, even if we don't think so.

When growing up we were told what we were supposed to do and who we were supposed to be in order to be accepted by our communities, our parents, our teachers, our peers, and our culture. The pressure immediately sets in and if we did not comply with the rules of these social norms, we were immediately judged, ridiculed, shamed, made fun of, often shunned, put down, and in the worse cases rejected by those people who were supposed to love, teach, and protect us. To avoid ridicule, shame, rejection, or the possibility of losing love, we put on masks, masks that hide our true selves.

Many of us hide behind our "public mask", the one we feel we need to show others that we are a perfect leader, wife, Christian, parent, family member, friend or that we are living a next to perfect life. At least that's how it was for me. I had a very successful 30-year career in the Navy, retiring as a Command Master Chief and at the military's highest enlisted pay grade of E-9.

I was able to visit many countries; meet wonderful people and did many things I may not, otherwise, have been able to do. I accomplished many things and was the "first" in several categories: first Woman of the Year in Sabana Seca, Puerto Rico, my first duty station; the first African American female Chief Petty Officer assigned as the Operational Test Director for Extremely High Frequency Satellite and Global Broadcast Service Programs; and the first African American female to persevere as Navy Region Japan's highest senior enlisted position as Command Master Chief, U.S. Naval Forces Japan, Navy Region Japan. While I was able to reach so many wonderful accomplishments, I must say it was not without internal pain and suffering along the way.

Many times, I felt like a fraud, trying to keep up appearances and pretending that everything going on with me was perfect. There was a period in my life where I wasn't sure how I was going to make it. I had become an expert on wearing masks, despite all the good things that were going on in my life, I knew I felt like my life from the outside was about to crumble.

I can remember this particular incident as clear as day, it was the day God used my daughter to save my life.

It was a Friday evening, at about 7:00 PM. I was home alone getting things prepared for the upcoming week. I was scheduled to travel to Cape Canaveral, Florida for a work assignment Monday and my mom was coming to my house Sunday to help take care of the kids while I was away. After I finished cleaning, laying out the kid's clothes for church and the upcoming school week I realized my daughter only had one pair of tights. Knowing she needed more, I decided to drive to Target before they closed to pick up a few pairs of tights that I know she would need for the week.

I got home from Target about 9:30 PM and there was a message on the answering machine. I hit play and the message instructed me to pick up my two children. I returned the call and asked if there was something wrong with my kids. The response was "no", but I needed to come pick them up because there was a change in his plans. This is when God gave me the first sign. I asked to have their coats on so I could come and go quickly. Then, before hanging up, I told him I was on my way and that, my two nieces were coming with me. That was a lie, I was alone, but I felt by saying I wouldn't be alone, I would be safe. I left my house and, as I was getting ready to shut the door, I paused and decided not to lock the door: this was the second sign. It took a total of about five minutes for me to drive to the apartment complex. As I pulled in, I decided not to pull into a parking space, but to instead park in front of the cars, effectively blocking them in, but leaving my car ready to pull off when necessary. This was the third sign.

I entered the apartment complex, knocked on the door and when the door opened, I noticed the apartment was dark. I didn't hear the kids, so I asked, where they were. He said they were sleeping in the bedroom. I quickly head straight to the bedroom, where the kids were sleeping, but did not have on their coats; the coats were stacked on the bed. As I put my daughter's yellow coat on her body, she remained asleep, she did not budge. Next, I reached for my son's coat and, as I did, my face encountered a fist and I fell against the wall, then to the ground. Dazed and caught off guard, I tried to get up, but couldn't, as the kicking wouldn't let me move further than a few inches. I began screaming and calling out for help.

As I screamed, "stop it, stop it", I curled up into a ball trying to protect whatever I could because I could literally feel every kick from head to toe. I remember trying to force myself up and when I did, I noticed the phone, not a cell phone but a house phone. I grabbed the phone to call 911 and as quickly as I reached for it, it was snatched out of my hands and I managed to get to my feet.

As I tried to get out of the small bedroom, I tripped over something, and fell down. While down, the kicking continued and, as I decided that I was going to get under the bed and hide, I heard someone shout, "stop it, stop it, stop it, stop it!" I look up and it was my daughter standing on top of the bed shouting. I then realized the kicking stopped, and I immediately went into survival mode. I got up, grabbed my daughter from the bed, grabbed my son with no coat on, and I ran with both kids as fast as I could. As we exited the apartment and headed to the car, I saw my car, not pulled into a parking spot but ready to pull off, I thanked God internally. I opened the door, my daughter climbs in and I get in with my son in my arms and pass him onto the passenger seat with his sister.

My adrenaline was flowing. As I pulled off, I tell my daughter, "when we get to the house you are going to have to get out of the car on my side. I will open my car door, grab your brother and get out of the car and then you will have to climb over the seat and get out". I tell her, "I will be carrying your brother so mommy is going to need you to run as fast as you can to open the door and hold it open for me and your brother". When we got home, I pulled into my driveway, I got out, locked the car door and as soon as that happened, I saw headlights coming fast around the corner. My daughter did as I asked and when we got to the house the door was unlocked just as I left it. I again, thanked God internally. We go in, I lock the door and no sooner than I do, the banging at the door begins. I run to make sure the back door is locked and begin checking the windows downstairs. As the knocking continues, I get both of the kids upstairs and lay down with them in my bed until the knocking stops. I am not sure what time the knocking stopped but when I realized it had, I get up to go see if the car was gone and that's when it hit me; I could barely move. My legs, my head, my back, my stomach, my arms, my side, my everything was in pain. I wasn't sure what to do so I decided to try soaking in the bathtub. As the bathwater was running, I reached under the cabinet for bubbles and saw the Epsom salt and decided to use that instead. I sat in that tub, crying and praying, praying and crying. It was then that I realized my daughter had saved my life.

When God is trying to tell us something, we should heed the warning signs. When I think back over that event, I can see that there were signs that God was showing me. It was as if He put a sign up that said "stop, danger, road closed", and a big "do not enter" sign in front of a huge barrier station. I failed to listen and drove right through that barrier station at a high rate of speed, ending up in a ditch after a horrible plunge.

After getting home that night I quickly thought about what others would think and if my neighbors heard any of what had just happened. What was I going to do in the morning, what was I going to say other than the truth, what lies was I going to tell, or excuses would I make? Those thoughts were coming from the mask I was wearing. The mask of perfection and pretense, never wanting anyone to know what happened to me. My physical body was bruised and hurt, but my mask of "perfection" and "pretense" was left untouched, it was still in its place, it had never been touched.

I witnessed the protecting power of God on this and many other occasions. Because He promised to protect me, He found a way for me to escape. I realized that if I had not left the car parked in that position or if I had not left my home door unlocked things would've been different.

What kept me going through turmoil was the fact that I had become an expert at wearing masks! I knew who I really wanted to be, the real me, but it was too hard to do because I was too busy trying to keep up appearances. I wanted to be real but did not know how. I was too consumed with what others would think. Those thoughts led to thoughts of feeling like a failure, being another statistic of divorce, another black woman with problems, etc. But that Friday night, God sparked a change in my soul that I couldn't overlook, something that I couldn't cover up and it wasn't easy to accept. When He woke my daughter up, He was using her to not only save my life, I believe He was using her to wake me up and do what was necessary to prevent her from becoming a part of the generational curse of abuse.

CHAPTER 2

❖ ✦ ❖

The Award Goes To......

> *"Authenticity is the daily practice of letting go of who we think we are supposed to be and embracing who we actually are."* - Brene Brown

It was fall and the beginning of my junior year of high school. I was 16 years old, traveling to Harrisburg, Pennsylvania to final auditions for a part in a play, it was about a 25-minute drive. The week prior, I made it past the first and second level of auditions in York, Pennsylvania, my hometown. As I stared out the window of the car looking at all the beautiful colors of the leaves, I didn't have a care in the world. My mom dropped me off at the entrance before she parked and, as I walked into the building, I began to feel nervous. I had never been in this particular, building, and when I walked into the room, I did not see any familiar faces. I never met the directors and was unfamiliar with the room where the auditions were being held. The script was nothing I read before, and as I took my seat to await instructions, I realized I was the only person of color in the room. There was nothing even slightly familiar to me. I refused to shutter, all of those unknowns made me more determined to outperform the other eight girls, I was determined to get the part. We were given 10 minutes to read over the script and memorize lines. When I was called, I walked into the room an entirely different person, I was in character mode. I left my nerves and all the things I was unfamiliar with outside that door and went right into my role. I could see it on their faces and in their body language, the directors were impressed and shocked that I memorized all of my lines and delivered a great performance.

The final audition was impromptu. We were not given a script, just a scenario. I don't remember exactly what the scenario was but what I do remember is it was dramatic. We had one take, and we had to include three different emotions. I went with my gut and did what came naturally, after all I practiced many times going from happy to sad, with full-blown snot and tears, in a heartbeat. I don't think they believed I could do it. I made it to the final set of auditions along with three others. But I was not selected for the part, they said they were looking for someone "a lot taller" and that I was too short.

Quite naturally, I was disappointed that I was not selected for the role, or asked to take another role, but there was a sigh of relief I felt inside. It was like a weight was lifted off of my shoulders, like the relief I felt when I began taking off my masks.

Acting is not much different than wearing a mask. Actors pretend – they imagine; and wearing a mask is quite similar. Both acting and wearing a mask is a matter of choice.

Whenever we don't want someone to know something or see something about ourselves, or when we want to hide something or pretend, it's like we're acting. The reality is, most people do it all day long.

When I told my mother I was going to write a book and what it was going to be about, she shared with me some of the things she learned from others about wearing a mask and pretending to be something other than your true self. She shared with me, what she learned after being around drug addicts. She started with a reminder that everyday people suffer with drug addictions and that they are around us, yet most of us don't even realize it. Addiction is a disease that the user is initially able to cover up, or mask, very well. It is a disease that is masked by politicians, teachers, lawyers, and everyday people who function in their daily lives without us noticing the disease until it has progressed, and by that time, it has resulted in serious behavioral changes, torn relationships, changes in physical appearance and sometimes death. She explained to me that we, their family members and friends, are often surprised and hurt when the "drug mask" is removed or has fallen off because the myth that addiction can never happen to "me" has been dispelled. The disease is not prejudice to gender, ethnicity, age, culture, background, profession, social status, etc.

She summed it up with frustration that she has seen people suffer from drug diseases in our black community. They were labeled as drug addicts and often ended up in jail. Now today, in white communities, the disease of addiction is called just that, a disease not an addiction, and they are sent to rehabilitation centers to get help fighting the disease. Her first point is, the same resources for persons, white or black, with drug addictions should be afforded the same resources. Her second point being, a drug disease addiction carries the same kind of deception as wearing a mask. The person wearing a mask and with the disease addiction is trying to convince others that what they are saying and doing is the absolute truth while pretending to be someone or something other than their true self.

There's a unique and distinctive power in knowing, becoming, and being your true self. Those who are truly happy in life understand this power and passionately strive to become their authentic selves.

Being true to yourself is not as simple as it may seem, especially for someone wearing a mask, or multiple masks, for any period of time. When we are in a situation or in an environment in which we are wearing our mask, there is one thing that is certain and that is, the truth always remains. To be true to yourself you must know who you are. To discover who you are, you must acknowledge you are wearing a mask, the type of mask you are wearing, then believe the mask must be removed and learn how to take it off. When that is done, we can begin being our true self.

Many years ago, as a young adult, I learned how to bind my anxiety, insomnia, depression, and worries behind a smile. That was my "smiling mask". I used my smile and external body language as a defense mechanism, trying my best to never let anyone see how I was truly hurting or the fact that I was struggling to handle the situation and things that were going on with me daily. In order for people to see who you really are, you have to show them what you're going through.

CHAPTER 3

<hr>

Understanding Authenticity: Knowing Yourself

"If we truly want to be remarkable you must first learn how to be yourself; this means living authentically with a deep sense of who you are and what you have to offer." – Matt Russell

---

A uthenticity is the key aspect of the value that you provide in words and in deeds. It's about presence, living in the moment with conviction and confidence, and staying true to yourself. A person who is authentic gives the people around them a welcoming feeling, makes them feel comfortable and at ease: something I observed in my paternal grandmother every time I was in her presence.

Authentic is defined as: "not false or copied; made or done the same way as an original." My favorite definition is" being true to one's own personality, spirit, or character."

On my first trip to Jamaica, my husband and I stayed at the Grand Palladium Resort for seven full days. There were so many things about the resort that I not only loved but will never forget: one of which was meeting a woman, we'll call her Tina.

My husband and I just finished having lunch at the Jamaican Jerk Hut and walked over to a well shaded section to enjoy the live band that was playing on the lawn. There were quite a few people on the lawn, and one of them was Tina. I met her earlier that morning in one of the resort stores, where we had a great conversation about the resort and our children.

About fifteen minutes after sitting on the lawn, Tina joined my husband and I, and we began having a light and casual conversation. She was the CFO for an organization in Houston, Texas. She was single, had two adult children, and four siblings – all of whom she was close to. She told me she was in Jamaica to "turn up" and take advantage of her time away from work and family. This was her time to let her hair down and relax. In her excitement, she told me that during her past three days at the resort she was able to truly be herself and not the way her boss, her peers or her family wanted or expected her to be. She said back at home she always felt stressed, smothered, over tasked, and unappreciated. Those feelings led to her being angry and resentful of her family and the people at work. For the next ten minutes she shared how she was feeling. Then she asked me, "do you understand what I'm saying, have you ever felt this way?" I paused, trying to think of what to say before I responded. I did not respond with a simple yes or no. Instead, I decided to respond with a statement and then ended my response with a question. I said, "Yes, I have previously felt over-stressed and over-tasked." Then I asked, "In what way have you tried talking to your boss or your family about your feelings?" She said she hadn't, but she clearly believed it was their fault that she felt that way because of all the work and demands they put on her. I asked her if she thought about telling her boss and family how she felt? She shared several reasons why she couldn't and after a few other open-ended questions, she said, "I think I need to start being honest."

I began sharing with her the practice of authenticity. I shared with her the power of choice; how often we underestimate the power of choice, and how it was okay to say no. She was afraid to share her true feelings with her family and her boss, who happened to be her friend. She was afraid they would become distant with her and, because of that, she kept her feelings to herself and pretended that all was well.

So, I asked her: 1. "If your family and your boss do not know you feel this way, how can they do anything to change?" She had no response. 2. "How do you expect change if nothing you say or do is different?" She had no response. 3. "Who needs to take action, you or them?" Her response was "me". She had so many feelings built up that she felt like she was about to explode with anger and frustration, yet the people she blamed for her feelings had no idea or any clue that she felt that way. I explained to Tina, her feelings of resentment and anger were based on her actions or her inability to act, by not telling her family and boss how she felt. I shared with her two of my favorite statements: people only do to you what you allow them to; and, we only know what people tell us. My last question to Tina was 4. "What action are you going to take?" She said her first step was to start being her true self, honest and open with herself and others.

We saw each other a few more times and before she departed, we exchanged contact information. That evening there was a fruit basket delivered to our room with a hand-written note of thanks.

We remain in touch today. She said she strives to stay mask free daily and is living authentically and completely happy doing so.

Authenticity is being true to yourself and others, not false and without imitation. To be authentic is to just be real. It might go without saying but to be true to yourself you need to know who you are and what you stand for. When you show up, you are who you are, nothing more and nothing less. It is so much easier to connect with others when we eliminate the pretense. One of the things that keeps us from being authentic is we are busy trying to be what people want us to be in order to be popular or accepted. When we are not being authentic, we are covering up what is going on within us and in our lives and sometimes that's our insecurities. Saying "NO" can be difficult for most people. I strongly encourage you to practice saying no. Look at yourself in the mirror and wholeheartedly say "NO" over and over until you are comfortable doing so.

Being authentic is having the courage to be imperfect, to be vulnerable and to set boundaries. Real authenticity requires self-monitoring and continual awareness of your thoughts, emotions, and behaviors.

My experience of building a business is not like any other experience I have encountered, and I would not change the decision to do so. There have been a lot of ups and downs and a whole lot of lessons learned throughout the process. About 4 years ago I was making plans to launch my business. My sister/ friend Simone was helping in the beginning stages and coaching me through the initial set up requirements. I chose Simone to guide me through this process over other sources because of her authenticity. I implemented her recommendations for setting up and launching my business and all of her input has paid off.

After the initial set up, I chose a website host and began to build content for the website. I must say, I truly thought I would have a final product within two weeks. I was wrong. I was fooling myself. I tried over and over again to convince myself that all of the time and effort I was putting into building the website was okay and that I could do this. I was wrong on so many levels. It seemed the more time and effort I put into the product the more there was for me to do. I had to finally face the facts and be honest with myself. I had to be truthful and authentic and admit that I could not do what I wanted or what needed to be done efficiently. I finally made a decision to contact a qualified company, set up a discovery call and while they were building all of the content for my website, I was able to totally focus my energy where it mattered – on my clients and the delivery of content. I should have applied a principle I use to follow while I was in the military: never operate or claim to speak about an area for which you are not qualified, go to the expert of that field. That simple decision to be honest with myself and walk in the authentic truth not only saved me time but a lot of energy.

In business, your authenticity comes through in your brand, your aesthetics, and your positioning. It's your platform to show your truth to your clients and the rest of the world. When a person is authentic or living in alignment with their true self, they are acting in ways that show how they genuinely feel. Being authentic requires that you know who you are and accept yourself for who you are. When you don't know who you are, what your beliefs are, what you stand for, or what your intentions are, you are living in a purposeless pursuit of happiness. Being authentic doesn't mean you are on a road to complete happiness. In fact, if you want to live a fulfilling life – not just simply a happy life – you need to answer the question "Who Am I?" And before you can answer that question, you have to learn to take off your masks.

When meeting with clients for the first time, I ask them this question: "Who are you?" The responses I always receive are, "I am the manager of the Sales team", "I am an HR Manager", "I'm a business owner", "I am an entrepreneur", or "I run a million-dollar consulting firm" and so on. The response they give always references their position or title. As my clients and I spend more time together and our work progresses, I'll ask that question again, and the responses change drastically. Given the nature of our work together, they begin to discover their identity and understand what they do is not who they are.

As a wife, a mother, a business owner, and especially as a leader, I have been asked numerous times about my goals. I have been asked about my dreams, my wants, and my desires. Specifically, I have been asked what my goals are and what plans I have for accomplishing those goals. I've been asked about my purpose and vision both personally and professionally. There is one question, however, no one seems to ever ask and that is "who are you?" Any Chief Petty Officer of the United States Navy can understand the importance of this question. The first time I was asked that question was September 15, 1996. I believe everyone should know who they are. Knowing who you are is the greatest wisdom anyone can possess. Know your goals, your morals, your values, what you love, your standards, what you will and will not tolerate. It defines who you are. As we grow older and interact with different people and experiences, who you are steadily evolves. If you are having trouble defining who you are, engage in self-reflection to uncover your truest self.

In my work with executives, I have found the mask metaphor to be relevant to both men and women.

I have witnessed these executives put on a mask of persona: toughness, boldness, happiness, sometimes leading a policy they may not have agreed with but were required to enforce as if they created it themselves.

Being authentic does not mean being perfect, but trying your best each and every day, walking the walk and aligning your actions with your words.

I can remember, as I was climbing up the ranks and began growing as a Senior Chief Petty Officer (SCPO), there weren't many female SCPOs at this particular command to bond with. I remained close friends with my fellow SCPO friends who worked at a different command. One of those friends shared with me a situation about the current command she was assigned to. She was given the responsibility to improve the performance and morale of her department. The majority of her department was young in age and in seniority. Her credibility was on the line, and with the little bit of information she had about her team, she wasn't sure they were up for the challenge. So, she put on the mask of toughness. This was not her natural leadership style, but she thought this was the logical approach, after all, she came from a male-dominated community and she thought this style would help her succeed. I can clearly remember our conversations during these difficult times. One evening, when she should have been home, she called me from her office and told me that she, "needed to vent." She said it was so hard leading this way because the Sailors in her department were doing whatever she asked of them and they were doing it well, but she was crushed inside because this was not her true self. She further shared that whenever her natural instincts and personality shined through with openness, warmth, and curiosity, she would suppress them back down for fear of not appearing to be soft or weak and not taken seriously. As a result, she created a dysfunctional work environment focused exclusively on execution and results. Finally, after the first three months, a mutual mentor of ours sat her down and told her to stop trying to be someone that she was not. He knew her well and she could not fool him. She had to drop the mask. When she did her department thrived and by the end of her three-year tour they soared in advancements, community service, qualifications, and off-duty education and overall performance.

Several years later she shared that story at her retirement ceremony. She said, "I wish I had listened to my instincts sooner instead of putting myself and my department through turmoil while pretending to be tough in a way that was neither necessary nor who I was." She further shared, "I was trying to be someone I wasn't and act in a way that was out of my character because I was trying to be all things to all people." Her best advice to all leaders, especially the junior Sailors was to "just know yourself and then be yourself."

Being authentic in leadership is not always easy, especially with so many competing requirements. Authenticity in leadership means the way we interact and act around others, regardless of the situation, should be aligned with our individual personality and principles. It means staying true to yourself. When you are truly authentic as a leader you are not afraid to show your emotions or show your vulnerability. That's what allows a leader to admit their mistakes and share lessons learned, while simultaneously re-membering to separate their emotions from the equation when making decisions.

There is a risk involved when we put ourselves out there personally and professionally. However, if we don't honor our true feelings and needs, they will eventually leak out, sometimes when we least expect it, and cause harm to oneself and others. The more we practice authenticity, the easier it becomes to live and lead from this place.

CHAPTER 4

─◆─❧◆✳◆❧─◆─

Alignment and Acceptance

> *"When you start doing things that are truly*
> *in alignment with what your true self wants,*
> *what your soul wants, you flourish, and life*
> *becomes a lot easier."*
> *—Joel Annesley*

My faith in God allows me to elevate my perspective beyond just what I see. It allows me to accept the past without living in it and move forward accepting who I am and aligning and accepting my truth. There are many circumstances that we hear and know about that we can't control. We hear about them on the news and the ones we experience in our everyday lives. A lot of times there's a story that we see and then there is the story that we tell ourselves. I think the story we tell ourselves plays a role in determining the pathway that we head in. We're either going to take the path of brokenness and bitterness or we're going to travel the path of restoration and redemption.

Even though I didn't ask for the events in my life to happen nor could I choose the circumstances of my story, I did choose my path, the path of restoration and redemption. That choice wasn't made by me because I'm so intellectual or so super saved, I was only able to make that choice because of the goodness and for-giveness God has given me and He's teaching me the importance and meaning of forgiveness. It's impossible to forgive another person unless you really understand how deeply you've been for-given. My relationship with God allows me to see that I have truly been forgiven of so many things. How can I not wholeheartedly forgive, after all, forgiveness is a loving thing to do?

The kindest thing I have ever done for myself was to forgive my-self and others. Actually, next to spending time alone with God, forgiveness has become one of my favorite things to do. It clears my way to move forward and it doesn't take time away from me – time that I will never get back while holding on to unforgiveness. It is then that the spirit can flow through me. I never thought for-giveness would bring me joy, but it has. It helps me stay aligned with my authentic self. I believe all forgiveness is self-forgiveness.

Wearing forgiveness as a mask, as a part of your daily attire, is not living in alignment with your authentic self. There are many forms of misalignment: masquerading as someone you're not, compromising what you feel is right, feeling strange in your own skin, masquerading for those around you. It's not hard to recog-nize. Your actions and behavior will not be settled within you. When you recognize what is causing the misalignment you have to take the necessary steps to realign both your true self with your actions and your integrity and your actions. You will need to identify and understand your passion, your purpose and walk in alignment with them both. Again, living authentically does not mean living perfectly; but as you walk in your authenticity remember to readdress as necessary.

You may wonder when you take off your mask will you still be viewed as important or as someone who has value? Will you still be important to your team, friends, family, or church? Will you be respected after you lose the masks full of color and design? Absolutely yes, and I talk more about dropping the mask in Part II. You will begin to be understood as you tap into the things that you have hidden and possibly never shown; your complete truth, your hurts, your pain, your guilt, your shame.

So how can you learn to become more authentic? We have to start by understanding why authenticity is important to you. Authenticity may be seen or felt personally as pretending or putting on a front. That pretense can shift from person to person and or from situation to situation. Inauthenticity is usually joined with feelings of deception, dishonesty, cheating, and fraud-like behavior. For many of us, that is usually our church or work personality. Sometimes inauthenticity appears as the person we "are" in relationships. Regardless of the persona you display, you can find a way to stray away from the person you are pretending to be. You can make sure your actions reflect who you truly are and ensure they are consistent with your character and values.

Authenticity has become an important value of mine. I grow my authenticity daily by loving myself enough to take the risk of showing myself – scars and all – to my friends, family, clients, and to the world. It can really be scary sometimes and fear often shows up right before I show my truth. Fear will say, "What if others don't love or accept this part of me?" I then ignore fear because no one is ever going to love or like everything about me and that's okay. I have decided to live life intentionally and fulfilling, starting each day anew. I continue opening doors, closets, and sharing these parts of me in skillful ways personally and professionally. Living authentically has become a way of life for me.

I get flooded with so much information each day. It can be overwhelming! I have to purposefully stay on top of my original schedule and plan, not letting meaningless conversations and individuals personal request creep into my agenda. It is easy to get off track and sometimes, whether you are aware of it or not, these things affect your desired results, thoughts, and outlook about different things. I have become intentional about not living in passive-mode, not accepting any and everything that comes my way. In its place, I approach each day visualizing I have an electronic in-box that accepts or rejects information based upon its contamination to my mental state. This allows me to be intentional about what occupies my precious mental space and allows me to continue walking in my authenticity.

I had a sorority sister once say to me, "you don't know yourself!" I thought to myself, who is she talking to? Not me! So, I calmly asked her, "why do you say that", she responded, "after I gave you the compliment you gave me a weird smile and moved on to the next conversation, never addressing the compliment given". She shared with me that my response was not the usual humble response I would give, but rather more of a shock, as if I was being told this information for the first time, and it was something I didn't know about myself. She explained that I should, with confidence, know the great quality traits that I consistently demonstrate. I thought about what she said and how much it really did relate to me knowing myself. Think about it, have you ever been in a conversation with someone who thinks more highly of you than you thought they did? Or the opposite, that they thought worse of you? Both have happened to me. Either way, how does the shock of that discovery or disconnect feel?

When you know yourself there is no presence of shock because there is no disconnect between what a person says and what you know to be true. When you know yourself, you are continuously maximizing your potential and living in your purpose. Knowing yourself is not a "how-to" step process, it happens incrementally. You are no longer trying to figure things out, no more guessing, no more hoping, and no more wishing.

PART II:

Rediscover Your Authenticity:
Unraveling The Inner Journey

CHAPTER 5

Inner Self vs Outer Self

"Your worst battle is between what you know and what you feel."
- Anonymous

O ne summer many years ago the kids and I traveled to Maryland to visit my aunt for a week. They were very young; in fact, both were under the age of four. They enjoyed visiting family and didn't seem to mind riding in the car to the various places we traveled. I'm sure it's because we sang, talked, laughed and we made a game of everything. I remember one night I became upset with my aunt because she had not been responsible in storing the many types of medicines she was prescribed. She would sit in this one chair, that was in the room where the kids would play, and that's where she would take her medicine. When she would finish taking the medicine, she had a habit of putting the bottles on the floor beside her chair. I asked her numerous times not to do this, but she would remember only for the next dose and afterward revert back to her bad habit. One night I was washing the dishes after dinner, I looked over the kitchen counter and saw the medicines scattered on the carpet and I got really angry. Like any parent, I was concerned about the safety of my children. What if they picked up that medicine, or ate the medicine? What if they got sick? What if I didn't notice the medicine spread all across the floor? But I kept quiet and I didn't say a word.

Suddenly, my daughter looked at me from the sofa and asked, "Mommy, why are you mad at Auntie?" Not knowing what to say, I kept quiet. But my aunt, who happened to be standing next to her husband, turned to my daughter and said, "Mommy is not mad at me. Why did you say that?" She affirmed her statement with a smile saying, "Yes, Auntie, mommy is mad at you." I was flabbergasted. I mean I was totally caught off guard by the way she discerned the situation. Although I had tried to mask my frustration and anger by remaining silent, my daughter had discerned the condition of my heart. She saw what I was feeling on the inside. This incident reminded me that God knows our hearts. He not only knows our hearts, but He is more interested in what is on the inside than what is on the outside.

In today's world, there seems to be a lot of focus on the outward image more so than the inward one. We do a lot of things to make sure we look good and present ourselves well. We ensure that any parts of our bodies – all things we don on, are in the best condition. We tend to lean more towards what is fake and deceiving with regard to our outward appearance. We invest a lot of time and money trying to mask or cover-up, who we really are, the real "us." We smile cheerfully while at work because we're afraid of what our colleagues or our boss might say if we don't. We chase what gives us more increase, glamour, or fame so that we look good on the outside at the expense of our inner self; all along creating inner conflict with ourselves. But the Lord made it clear that the outside is not what matters to Him when He told Samuel: "Do not look at his appearance or at his physical stature, because I have refused him. For the Lord does not see as man sees; for man looks at the outward appearance, but the Lord looks at the heart" (1 Sam 16:7, KJV).

Kids learn how to improvise at a young age, at least I know we did in our household and in our neighborhood. In the winter months it snowed a lot but that did not keep us inside the house. When we didn't have sleighs to ride down the snowy hills with, we used large pieces of cardboard. If we didn't have 10 jacks to play with, we would use small pebble stones. When we wanted to make the room a different color we would place a shirt over the lampshade to change the color and brightness of the light. We let our minds roam free back then. We did not seem to let anything stop us from having fun or making the best of our situation. We were without conflict between our inner and outer self, we seem to just live life carefree.

When someone looks at us, before we say one word, they only see our physical outside being. If we haven't learned to live authentically, when we present ourselves, they see a masked person. Why? Because we think our masks will protect us. Protect us from our fears of being found out, fear of our secret selves being revealed and out in the open. But our mask blocks the shine of our inner light, our inner self. Our true self is within and it shines like a light. It makes things clear and in order for it not to be seen it has to be physically turned off or covered up.

When the inner self and the outer self are not the same it becomes unbalanced or in conflict. The inner self, your core, knows what is right and the outer self relies on action, what we do. Like any conflict, this conflict between our inner and outer self has to be resolved or at least managed.

I believe as children we were our truest self. With age we get so conscious of what people think of us and how we should present ourselves in a crowd or on the internet. That's when the outer self comes into play, that's when we put on the mask. Take off the mask, forget the outer self and focus on your inner self. Eliminate the conflict between the inner and outer self by quieting the outer self and become intentional about letting your truest self, your inner self, shine brightly. When your inner self is congruent with your outer self it will be just like looking in the mirror smiling, happy to see the real you.

The apostle Paul believed that our character was not determined by external appearances. He wrote, "When I was a child, I spoke as a child, I understood as a child, I thought as a child; but when I became a man, I put away childish things" (1 Cor.13:11). He made it clear that maturity has very little to do with our age, size, height or looks; but it has to do with what's inside, what's in our hearts.

CHAPTER 6

━━◆ ⊰◊⊹❋⊹◊⊱ ◆━━

Hold Up Your Mirror

"Learning without reflection is a waste. Reflection without learning is dangerous." – Confucius

There was a mirror that hung in the hallway of my godparent's' home. It was beautiful and always clean. It seemed extremely large with a thick heavy wooden frame. You had to pass the mirror whenever you came into the house or when you were leaving the house. Everyone seemed to love this mirror, but no one loved it more than my godmother. If I was leaving the house in haste, I remember my godmother would say, "pause and take time to look yourself over before you walk out the door." I'm sure I glanced into the mirror as I walked toward the door, but she wanted me to slow down, and do what she called a "once over". Making sure everything was in its right place, my hair, my clothes, my shoes, clean nose, moisturized lips, etc. I would do as she said but would still scurry out the door. I must have been in the sixth grade, too young to take myself se-riously because I don't remember ever making any adjustments.

Fast forward twenty years, I would look into the mirror and see all my imperfections. My eyes would meet in the mirror and I could see my extra baby weight, the scar on my face, the freckles that were beginning to appear, and my non-existent waistline. I would feel disappointment overcome me as I would walk away, walk away wearing a mask.

One of my favorite leadership books is "The 15 Invaluable Laws of Growth", by John C. Maxwell. The third law in the book is The Law of the Mirror, followed by The Law of Reflection, how fitting. The Law of the Mirror says, "You Must See Value in Yourself to Add Value to Yourself." This entire chapter is filled with so many nuggets that apply to personal and professional growth. John says, "I set cause for you to look within and be honest with yourself and help you discover who you are meant to be by God."

"Our lives only improve when we are willing to take chances and the first and most difficult risk, we can take is to be honest with ourselves." ~Walter Anderson

- **Self-Honesty**

We have to begin looking within ourselves and be honest about what we see. How do we respond or react to certain comments or actions? The way we respond or react is a reflection of what is in our hearts. To make any lasting change or practice self-aware-ness we need to examine ourselves. The only way we can truly examine ourselves is to be brutally honest with ourselves.

- Self-Discovery

Personal action follows self-honesty. When entering a 5K run for the first time you have to decide to finish. Whether you slowly travel across the finish line or you sprint across, both accomplish the same goal: crossing the finish line and both will change the way you look at organized running. Your self-discovery is something that can only be done by you. After learning from successes and failures, searching internally and being honest with yourself, you have to decide to move forward and travel on the road to self-discovery.

Through mentoring and coaching I knew two people who truly hated their jobs and the work they were doing – one male one female. The male had been out of college one year and the female had a husband and three children. They were both working at jobs that paid extremely well with great insurance and benefits packages, but they hated the work they were doing. Slowly, the lack of satisfaction began to take a toll on their health and happiness. Instead of pursuing their dreams, they stayed at those jobs because of complacency and sometimes to please their parents or others. They were possibly wearing the mask of "The Compliant Son" or "The Good Provider" and it hurt them. After a period of time, they both left the safe zone and began pursuing their dreams and walking in their purpose. Today, they are both entrepreneurs running lucrative businesses. They took a chance on themselves, kicked pretense out the door and began doing the work they were passionate about. Life can certainly pull us in many directions and create all kinds of pressures for us to be a certain way and do certain things. However, at the end of the day, the fact is we have to live our lives and we deserve to live them on our own terms even if it means disappointing others.

I have also known people who felt trapped and miserable within relationships where their partner did not honor their hopes or their dreams. They reluctantly wore "The Happy" mask to keep up appearances when they were actually feeling sad, lonely, and frustrated. This situation can literally be crushing to the soul and yet the pressure to stay in that relationship is what kept them trapped. It's very challenging to live life with passion when you are disrespected and put down on a regular basis. It's unhealthy. Continuing to wear the mask of "The Good Wife" or "The Good Husband" should be based on each person honoring their partner fully with love and respect.

It seems to me when most of us look into the mirror we are looking for reassurance and self-worth, yet we all are not able to look at ourselves in the mirror objectively.

I must admit, I use to look in the mirror and see every fallacy, even the ones I could not physically see but existed in my mind. Not today. Now when I look into the mirror I see all of my beauty and my greatness - they overpower my past flaw.

Like masks, mirrors come in many different styles and shapes. They can be smooth, shiny, come with glitz, glitter, and other shiny objects. When we are honest with ourselves and know who we are, we can use them both for their true purpose.

It may be considered bad luck, but when mirrors break the reflection remains unchanged.

CHAPTER 7

⊰ ⊱

Guard Your Mind

> "In order to live in the reality of our God's given destiny, you must consistently guard your mind against all self-defeating thoughts." – Edmond Mbiaka

One of the best books I have ever read is "Battlefield of the Mind" by Joyce Meyer. When I was reading this book, I began studying the written material. I was taking notes, looking up scriptures, and highlighting throughout the text. This book was full of such valuable nuggets of information that I went back through the book a second time just to review all the highlighted, circled, and underlined text. There was something about the stories and scriptures she shared that really resonated with me. I was able to relate to each of the conditions she addressed: worry, doubt, confusion, depression, anger, feelings of condemnation, and how to fight all these conditions. As she addressed each of these, it was clear that it all came down to one thing: the battlefield starts with you and your way of thinking. I was able to see what was going on in my mind and how little control I had over my mind. So many of us walk around defeated and try to carry the weight of the world on our shoulders, thinking we can never overcome our struggles. The bible says, "I thank God through Jesus Christ our Lord. So then with the mind I myself serve the law of God; but with the flesh the law of sin." (Rom 7:25, KJV). It is with the mind we serve the Lord. The mind is the battleground, the place where the greatest conflict exists.

As I continued to read the way I was feeling shifted, taking me to a different place. It was like being on the flight deck of a Navy aircraft carrier and being catapulted. I was learning to walk in my truth while understanding I was not alone. I was learning to be authentic.

It was not only a way to live, but instead, the more authentic I was proved that it was the only way to live. The steps to authentic living was forcing myself to become more aware of what I was and was not doing. As I did, I began to understand the power of my mind and focused more on what I was feeding my mind. I recalled a statement my old bible study mentor, Arzada Hines -whom I love, honor and respect - use to say all the time: "The mind is the most powerful asset that we all have. Don't underestimate it!" Years later, when I was reading Battlefield of the Mind, I began to understand what she meant by that statement. The mind can either make or break us, it has the power to build or destroy. Either way, the choice lies within us, we have the power, we have to take control over what we allow to get into our minds, it's our choice. While studying this book I began being intentional about my everything; my overall well-being, my surroundings and my productivity.

After being in the military for 30 years, 20 of which were served in leadership positions, I have witnessed, counseled, and helped many people overcome traumatic situations. I can remember one story that struck a nerve with me then and the feeling has not changed. It's a story I once told my friend Trina. A Second-Class Petty Officer was going to a basketball game with her boyfriend, they both loved the game. They were going to watch the base tournament playoffs. She and her boyfriend knew players from both teams, but she was supporting her co-workers' team. It was a good game that went into overtime. After the game they walked off the bleachers and began walking out of the gym, she saw her co-worker from across the gym floor and called his name, "Dance", she yelled. Dance looked back and gave a thumbs up. She waved and with excitement, she said "congratulations!" She continued walking out of the gym with her boyfriend side-by-side. They got into the car, the boyfriend was in the driver's seat and she was in the passenger seat. She began putting on her seat-belt and as soon as she clicked it into place, she felt a blow to her upper left jaw. Her hands immediately went to her face, but it was too late to block the blow. With confusion, she began to wonder what had just happened. While crying she asked, "what was that, why did you do that?" Her boyfriend's reply, "don't ever embarrass me by calling another man's name when you are with me."

They drove in silence. The car ride home was less than 15 minutes. As she was crying, she looked in the mirror, praying there was no evidence of what had just happened, that there would be no bruises visible. Those prayers went unanswered as the swelling and marks were already present. As they drove to his apartment, he began his apologies about the swelling and the marks, yet he never once apologized for the stupid reason he hit her. Within the next hour, she could see the marks under her woke up. When she woke up the next morning to get ready for work, the swelling had gone down but there was no guessing, she had a black eye. She was trying to figure out what she was going to say when she got to her office, how she was going to explain her eye and what lies she would tell to keep from telling the truth.

She called her job and told them she was going to be late because she had been in a car accident. That was lie number one. In the meantime, she went to the drug store trying to find some conceal-er to cover up the black eye, after all, she had already forgiven her boyfriend, and she needed her co-workers and friends to see he was a great, gentle, and loving man. He was the first guy to ever court her and she thought he was perfect. She convinced herself that this was an isolated incident. When she got to work she was bombarded with question after question and with every question came lie after lie. She was wearing a very vibrant mask. The mask of perfection. The mask that said nothing was wrong, I'm good, I don't have drama, I am in a great relationship and I am still an out-standing Second-Class Petty Officer. This mask was one of pro-tection, a mask of defense, after all she was defending her abuser.

We lie, tell half of the truth, or stay quiet because we are not sure what will happen if we share what is going on or how we feel. That girl, the Second-Class Petty Officer, experienced soreness, headaches, and restless nights because of the abuse of her boy-friend. Sometimes the evidence of abuse is not always as obvious as the physical injuries left by physical violence. A lot of pain and suffering comes from emotional abuse which doesn't always leave physical marks.

You only know what people tell you. For some people sharing their stories of physical abuse is the most difficult thing they have ever done. In fact, some survivors still cannot talk about their experience of abuse. For me it can be somewhat painful, but it is even harder and more painful to keep inside. I have numerous stories of abuse and I am blessed to be someone who has survived and come out on the other side safely. I believe sharing our stories with others will help at least one person.

Your mind is responsible for reasoning and thinking. Along with your emotions lie your feelings, and with that, your will to make decisions and choices. You get to guard your mind and decide who and what influences you – how you think, how you feel, and what you do. You get to decide what you let in and what you don't. You are the air traffic controller of your mind and you decide what plane is going to land. You decide what thoughts are going to take resident in your mind. Different thoughts come to us all the time. Some horrible, bad, good, and wonderful. So, decide what you will and will not let into your mind. The Bible says, "every high thing that exalted itself against the knowledge of God and bringing into captivity every thought to the obedience of Christ. (2 Cor 10:5 NIV).

CHAPTER 8

━◆◦✦◦◦◆━

The Sweet Spot

> *"The magic happens when you find the sweet spot where your genuine interest, skills, and opportunity intersect. - Scott Belsky*

I love to begin my day early in the morning. Most people would say I am a morning person. In fact, my husband and son, who are also morning people tell me I am an over the top morning person because I am ready to engage in conversation as soon as I wake up. When I was stationed in Yokosuka, Japan I loved getting up super early because the sun would rise about 4:00 am. I would get up at 4:15 am every morning and either go for a run at 4:30 am or take a fitness class from 5:00 am - 6:00 am. When I would get home from my workout, everyone would be up getting ready for work and school. I was fully energized but no one else wanted to engage in conversation. In fact, it wasn't until years later that they told me they didn't like when I would try talking to them early in the morning. They said I was too wound up in the morning and that my talking irritated them. When I thought about it, I had already been awake for about two hours when they were just waking up and beginning their day. I had to find a balance between honoring their morning wake up time and my two-hour head start.

Now, being an empty nester, I can appreciate and understand their sentiment. I love the darkness of the morning, the quiet time to be alone with God, no one needing me for anything. By the time my children would come downstairs, everyone was awake and ready to engage in conversation, talk about their events for the day. It took me a while to realize this was the sweet spot for my morning routine.

The sweet spot is like finding balance. As related to this book, the sweet spot is that place where your greatest self-awareness, your highest personal growth, and your genuine relationships/ connections with others meet. It is where the arena is stress-free and where comfort and peace live. Finding this place came after I learned about the mask I wore and after I began looking into the mirror and being honest with myself. Through this self-reflection, I discovered the significance of the sweet spot; personal growth, self-awareness and genuine relationships with others.

The significance of personal growth: Personal growth is like authenticity; it is not a final destination it is a journey. It's a continual process of learning that begins early in life and doesn't end at any particular age. Moreover, like authenticity, personal growth can help you in every area of your life. It allows you to take chances and step out of your comfort zone. As a result of focusing on personal growth, I have a better understanding of myself and I'm always pushing to another level of potential.

The significance of self-awareness: Self-awareness is being in touch with your thoughts, beliefs and your emotions, paying attention to what is going on around and inside of you. It means knowing your feelings, values, personality, needs, habits, emotions, strengths, weaknesses, fear, etc. Self-awareness helps you see who you truly are and connect with yourself in an authentic way. Being authentic is not about being perfect but about being you, your true self, in all aspects of your life.

The significance of relationships with others: being open and honest with yourself and others is the key to healthy relationships and connections. After we accept and understand our authentic self, the one in the mirror, our failures, insecurities and all, we can begin making connections with people and building genuine and meaningful relationships. Building real relationships with people is important for survival. It is important that we nurture and grow healthy connections with others. A perfect example is the relationship my husband and I have with Dr. Newton and Kimberly Miller. It is one that encourages trust, peace, love, friendship, and great energy. Relationships that are healthy mentally and emotionally should make you feel safe, satisfied, supported, and connected.

There was a period of time when I was busy keeping busy. There was always something to do or somewhere to be. Keeping busy was a way of keeping distracted from the mask I was wearing. Keeping busy allowed me to identify the mask I wore, while taking them off and learning to be authentic gave me a sense of awareness and presence. I was able to acknowledge my feelings and learn to process through them, and the more I acknowledged my feelings the more natural it became. I felt awake and alive and as I learned more about myself, I discovered my sweet spot, the balance.

Today when I am busy, I don't look at the busyness in a flustered, panicking, or overwhelming way. I am now able to live a more balanced and satisfying life even in the middle of my busyness, making things for me calmer, peaceful and relaxed. Always ready to drop the mask.

CHAPTER 9

Dropping the Mask

> *"For a seed to achieve its greatest expression, it must come completely undone. The shell cracks, its insides come out and everything changes." ~Cynthia Occelli*

Have you ever thought about the process of a chicken laying an egg? When I was younger, I attended a summer camp at the York Rescue Mission, Monday thru Friday. They would take us on different trips at least three times a week. When we traveled to small farms, I often asked questions about the chickens. "How did the baby chick get into that shell? How does the shell break open, does the mother chicken use her nose to break it open? Does the shell hurt the baby chick?" I learned that the shell keeps the chick safe before the hatching begins and that the process of hatching does not hurt the baby chick at all. In fact, once the chick is hatched, it has no use for the cracked and damaged shell.

The memory of that story helps me relate the hatching of the egg to the removal of masks. The shell gets cracked, breaks, and falls completely off the baby chick. The shell is like our mask, our outer part. When we shed our mask, we let go of our hurts, shame, fear, pain. Our outside is cracked and broken but our inside, who we truly are, remains undamaged.

When wearing masks, we worry about what we are showing others, the outer part of our being. We don't worry about the inward parts. As we let go of the masks and begin to rediscover ourselves, we realize there can be something liberating about that process.

Hiding behind a mask whether it's our job title, church ministry, political status, clothes, or our role at a non-profit organization – it can be exhausting. At some point you can get so tired, possibly frustrated and overwhelmed with keeping up the facade that the mask can feel heavy. And like a pair of shoes, the mask can lose its shape, comfort, and form. It can become worn and when it does you must take it off. If you are ready to take off your masks don't overthink it, just do it. Allow authenticity to lead the way of this very self-rewarding place of living mask free.

Taking off masks was something I had to learn by doing. Below are a few strategies that have worked for me and may also work for you.

1. **Become aware** that you are wearing a mask. The first step is to become aware that you are wearing a mask of some sort. Until you do that, nothing else can be done. Once you become aware that you are wearing a mask you can then move forward with taking the mask off.

2. **Recognize** what mask you are wearing. What mask are you wearing to hide your true self? The perfect one, the smiles, fear, shame, fashionista, diva, arrogance, innocence, toughness, etc. What is it that you try to be? happy, bold, dumb, social, etc. Regardless of the mask or masks you are wearing, take some alone time to self-reflect, get to know yourself and be honest with yourselves. It is the one way to move forward on the path of self-discovery.

3. **Acknowledge** that your mask is not who you are. Accept and acknowledge your internal feelings, don't avoid them. This will cause you to be vulnerable, and that's okay. Admit to yourself what is going on inside of you and begin to walk in your authenticity.

4. **Decide** to be you. Follow your personal values and authentic self. Allow the people around you the chance to get to know the real you and recognize and celebrate your God-given strengths and limitations.

5. **Take action,** take off the mask. This may be painful to do, but it is doable. Take off your mask and show the world who you really are. Be true to yourself and let your life be free, free to be who God called you to be.

Today is the day, it's your day to take off your mask. You can do it one step at a time. As you peel back each layer, you will discover your true self and reveal who you were created to be. Get excited about this journey as you fall in love with your true self and showcase the person beneath the mask.

Believe in yourself. Take off the mask!

Several years ago, one of my college professors had the class read the poem "Please Hear What I'm Not Saying" in its entirety. I remember before we began discussing the reading assignment he read the poem out loud to the class. This poem made a lasting impression on me. I remember how challenged I was, how I thought my professor must have been sent on an assignment from God to reveal this poem to me. As I spent time reading and reflecting on the poem, my emotions were all over the place. This poem sparked something in me personally and professionally, I knew I had to stop faking, I had to be consistent and live my life with purpose and meaning. I had to admit and recognize the mask I was hiding behind and take the risk to do something about it.

Excerpt from the Poem "Please Hear What I'm Not Saying" by Charles Fin

> Don't be fooled by me.
>
> Don't be fooled by the face that I wear. For I wear a mask.
>
> I wear a thousand masks that I am afraid to take off, and none of them is the real me.
>
> So, don't be fooled by me, I'm good at pretending.
>
> I give the impression that I'm cool and confident, but inside, it's different.
>
> I'm not in command.
>
> I'm often confused, lonely and desperately need someone to understand me.

But I hide and I don't want anyone to know.

That's why I frantically create a mask to hide behind,

I'm afraid to show the real me.

I'm afraid that you will not accept me.

I'm afraid that you will think less of me and laugh at me.

You see, deep down, I'm afraid that I'm nothing, that I'm no good,

And if you knew me, you would reject me.

So I play my game, my pretending game, and thus begins my parade of masks.

My life becomes a front to protect the real me.

I chatter idly to you about everything but tell you nothing of what's going on inside me – my fears, my worries, my doubts.

So when I'm talking, please listen carefully and try to hear what I'm not saying, what I'd like to say but I can't.

I'd like to be genuine, honest and sincere, but I cannot with-out your help.

My trust grows very slowly, so you will have to be patient with me.

Each time you are kind, gentle and encouraging, each time you try to understand, I am given new hope and I start believing in myself in a new way.

You let me see its o.k. to be me.

So I can take off the mask and be happy in your company, I can let you see the real me.

Who am I you may wonder? I am someone you know very well.

For I am every man and woman you meet

That self will remain buried until a time when he or she encounters unconditional love without and within. The final lines of the poem are a wake-up call for us all. We all wear a thousand masks and that it is only the person without the masks who creates the opportunity for others to become real, authentic, and unconditionally loving. As a society, we appear to face quite an uphill struggle to create relationships that foster being real, rather than being masked.

PART III:

Renew Your Authentic Self: Rebuilding Your Identity

CHAPTER 10

✦⟡✳⟡✦

Start From Where You Are

> *"It's like, remember who you always were, where you came from, who your parents were, how they raised you. Because that authentic self is going to follow you all through life, so make sure that it's solid so it's something that you can hold on and be proud of for the rest of your life."* – Michelle Obama

It was over. She was gone. My mind was filled with mixed feelings that were traveling 80 miles per second. The heartache for the loss of my best friend who was more like my sister was beginning to rise up within me. The first six weeks following her death I was so busy tending to others and avoiding the reality of her loss that I did not have time to work through or deal with my feelings. It all happened so fast. I didn't make time to deal my feelings because I was too busy thinking of her children, her mother, sisters, and the rest of her family. Six weeks later, I was back in Florida, back at work and feeling so many emotions that I was still trying to mask.

First anger settled in. I thought, how dare he? How could he be so selfish and full of lies? Next, there was pain. My heart, my feelings, and my soul all seemed to be so heavy, I felt lost. Then there was loneliness. I wanted to reach out to one person, the one friend I knew could carry me through this emotional whirlwind. Her baby sister and my dearest friend Valerie. Yet I couldn't call her, I was too worried about putting my emotions on her, I was afraid of setting her back.

Any defining moment in our life is an occurrence or a situation where we must make a choice. We decide whether that moment becomes a catastrophe or a breakthrough opportunity. Seeing missteps, mistakes, failures, missed opportunities as opportunities for growth, shifts your view. You go from that of a victim where life is happening to you, to someone who can face any challenge, rise, and use the obstacles of life as motivation and energy, to move forward, to start from where you are.

After we drop the mask and begin renewing our authentic self and rebuilding our identity we have to start from where we are. Drive and determination coupled with that newfound motivation and energy to start from where we are will help you travel the road to personal and or professional success. It all begins with one step followed by another step. No matter who you are, where you are from, your occupation, or where you are in life, you have enough strength inside of you to take that first step.

Arthur Ashe was a professional tennis player who was known for his quickstep which led to his winning of three Grand Slam titles. He remains the only black male tennis player to win the singles at Wimbledon, the U.S. Open, and the Australian Open. He also lived with a mask; he hid behind the mask of illness.

After he came forward with the news of his health battle, he was able to take the mask off. He was finally free from the burden of trying to hide his condition. He was living mask free. One of his famous quotes was, "Start where you are. Use what you have. Do what you can." This quote is about the simple truth. By working with what you have you collect more experience and find what you're good at. In the end, you'll be able to do much more than you thought possible. In order for anyone to get anything or anywhere in life you have to simply start from where you are. Arthur Ashe understood this very well. In addition to his tennis career, he was an activist who fought for several causes, civil rights, education, apartheid, and AIDs. He was the best version of himself and did the best he could in order to make life better for anyone he could. He dropped the mask and started from where he was, he used what he had, and he did what he could.

It comes as no surprise to my family how much I admire sports figures Arthur Ashe and Muhammad Ali. Both were vulnerable as well as transformational activists who pushed the nation toward freedom and democracy. They set an example that so many of us can learn from by turning vulnerability into strength - and vulnerability can be a tricky thing.

I use to believe vulnerability was a sign of weakness and that it was related to a lack of self-confidence. It was something that I tried never to display in front of others because I thought in order to be vulnerable, I had to bear all, reveal everything. I learned through various obstacles in my adult life that that is not true. Vulnerability is speaking the truth and it does not have to include "telling your life story". I am so glad that my original mindset regarding vulnerability did not stick with me. I am so glad that my mindset regarding vulnerability did not stick with me, I learned through various obstacles in my adult life that that is not true.

You may have heard Brene' Brown speak or maybe you've read one of her books. If you have not, I highly recommend you do so. She is a professor, researcher, best-selling author, writer, and TED talk speaker. Brene' defines authenticity as "a collection of choices that we have to make every day. It's about the choice to show up and be real. The choice to be honest. The choice to let our true selves be seen." She says, "vulnerability is the birthplace of connection and the path to feeling of worthiness. If it doesn't feel vulnerable, the sharing is probably not constructive," and "vulnerability sounds like truth & feels like courage. Truth and courage aren't comfortable, but they are never weakness." Vulnerability is about showing up, being honest, and letting ourselves be seen even when we can't control or predict the outcome.

Here is a great application of vulnerability. My dear friend, who also happens to be my sorority sister recently experienced the loss of someone she loved and was extremely close with. It came as a surprise and was a huge setback for her. Several weeks after her loss, I asked her how she was doing. She paused, then told me that she started to deliver the standard response of choice and not of feeling by saying "I am doing fine." A response to avoid any expression of vulnerability. The problem is, that response was not a true. She knew she wouldn't be fooling anyone, not even herself.

Then she said she wanted to feel free, she no longer had the desire to pretend, she wanted and needed to respond honestly by sharing how difficult everything was going for her. Responding in this way did several things for her. It immediately deepened our connection with one another, it put her at ease, and it helped with h grieving and healing.

Trying to get back to our authentic self can almost always be confronted with perfectionism and comparison. Trying to be perfect and comparing ourselves to others is a goal we should not strive for, it's a battle we should not fight, it's a race we will not will.

There was a crow that lived in the woods. He was happy with his life and never wanted for anything. Then one day the crow saw a dove and thought, "That dove is so beautiful and bright, I am so dark and dull compared to the dove." The crow went to the dove and said, "You are so beautiful. You must be the happiest bird alive." The dove said, "I use to think I was the happiest bird alive until I saw the robin. Its chest was so red and vibrant, I feel so plain. I think the robin is the happiest bird alive." So, the crow approached the robin and said, "You are so beautiful, you must be the happiest bird alive." The robin said, "I thought I was the happiest bird alive until I saw the peacock. Its colors were so unique, striking and gorgeous. My red chest looks so boring compared to the peacock, I think the peacock is the happiest bird alive." So, the crow flew to the zoo to meet the peacock. There were crowds of people surrounding the peacocks' cage taking pictures. When the crowd left, the crow said to the peacock, "You're so beautiful, you must be the happiest bird alive." The peacock sighed and said, "I thought I was the happiest bird alive but then they put me in the cage because of my beauty. When I look up to the sky and see crows flying free. I think the crow is the happiest bird alive." When we compare ourselves to others, we lose sight of our God-given talent, gifts and blessings.

Sometimes we look to people for inspiration. Inspiration is fine, but not for comparison, the comparison is only good as far as what we see in the public arena.

People share online, on their social media profiles, they post pictures or videos of them having the best times, eating fancy meals, their accomplishments, the nice holidays and the kids playing, dancing and singing. What most people don't share, or rarely share, is their reality, the things that are not going so well: their difficult times, when the kids are being rebellious, unhappy times with their partner, the bad times that offset the good times. Those comparisons are unhelpful, and they rob you of happiness, gratitude, joy, and fulfillment. Nothing good ever comes from comparing ourselves to others. God gave us one life to live, we were not born to live someone else's life. You have to decide to shift your mindset and get control of where you are and where you want to be.

Don't try to be better than anyone else. Focus on being a better version of yourself than you were yesterday. If you stumble, it's okay, brush yourself off and try again. Remember, take baby steps and you will reach your desired destination.

We cannot control what other people say, think or do. We can, however, control our reactions to the things they say, think and do. I learned this lesson when my best friend was murdered. She was the most loving person I have ever met. I had to decide to do my best, be there for her loved ones, and allow others to do the same for me. I had to face my fears and deal with the reality of her loss. I asked God to keep us along the way and for 21 years He has.

I hope you, and I, will be brave enough to live our lives in ways that promote wellness through authenticity and vulnerability, so that in the end, we can experience a life of joy and whole-heartedness. Tapping into our authentic selves is something we have to continually work towards, it is a never-ending process. We have to get out of our own way.

CHAPTER 11

Get Out Of Your Own Way

> "There are plenty of difficult obstacles in your path. Don't allow yourself to become one of them. – Ralph Marston

B lake's Kitchen. From a young age, my friend Blake had a dream of becoming a chef, and that was the name he was going to give his restaurant. Growing up he would always talk about how he wanted to open a restaurant and cook different types of food. He spent a lot of hours pretending to cook and then his parents allowed him time in the kitchen to practice cooking and serving his family. When Blake was in his teens, his mother insisted he spend more time playing outside with his friends. After he received a barely average report cared, she insisted he spend more time studying. She told him, "cooking is a nice hobby", but he needed to learn how to do more than cook.

As time passed, Blake spent more time with his friends and studying. He realized he was good at Science, Technology, Engineering, and Mathematics (STEM) subjects. He told himself he could make good money in the STEM career field. He went to college and became a chemical engineer and landed a job that paid very well, but he still wanted to open that restaurant. He told himself he would work for 10-12 years, save money, and open that restaurant. As time passed, the excuses for following his plan to open his restaurant grew. When the company he worked for closed, he began looking for a new job. This is when he began thinking hard about his dreams, but he hadn't saved any money or completed any research about opening a restaurant. He then realized he had to stop with the excuses, stop procrastinating, and begin working toward his dream. As he began to invest in his dream it became clear how his excuses were the biggest obstacle standing in the way.

Speaking from my own experiences, "getting out of your own way" means your behavior, actions, habits, thoughts, etc., are creating obstacles to your progress or your own success. If there is something "in your way" it's stopping you from moving. If a tree falls in the road after a heavy storm, that tree has to be moved in order for you to move forward. You are that tree, you have to be moved out of your own way so you can progress and work towards your goals, dreams, and renew your authentic self.

The only one stopping you, blocking you, is you. It's not your education, it's not your bank account, lack of opportunity, it's not your friends or family, or lack of resources. You are the only person standing in your way on the path to greatness. Unfortunately, we often can't see our blind spots, we don't notice our limiting beliefs. Sometimes we aren't aware of our self-destructive behaviors.

During my 30 years in the military, I experienced a lot of changes. Changes in jobs, policies, programs, and locations. I have moved from city to city, from state to state, from continent to continent and from country to country. I think I can say with full confidence, moving to a new location does not change you. Moving doesn't automatically make you better than you were in your previous city, state, country or continent. Moving or changing locations also doesn't make you any better than the people who were in your last, city, state, continent or country. In order for things to become different, change has to happen and if there is a personal change that needs to happen that change has to come from within you. You have to recognize that there needs to be a change and have a mindset shift. You have to work on things or apply the things that have an impact on the change you're trying to make as you renew your authentic self.

I am an optimistic person and I believe there is truth in the cliché, "where there is a will, there is a way." I truly believe that no situation is ever hopeless, nothing in life just happens, you have to make it happen. It is important to have a dream and pursue it with everything you have. But I haven't always thought this way. I was a worrywart, somebody who constantly worries about so many things. This was yet another part of my behavior that I covered up from everyone except my son who took notice of my unnecessary worrying.

"Worry is a thin stream of fear trickling through the mind. If encouraged, it cuts a channel into which all other thoughts are drained." — Arthur Somers Roche

I wish I could say I have no idea when or how it all began, but that would be untrue. My worrying came as a result of anxiety. This anxiety was triggered when working for an old boss who was pompous, arrogant and very self-serving, I will talk more about this later. I had become a habitual worrywart as a result of my constant over-thinking, thinking about things I had no control over. I was filled with worry and thoughts about what should have, could have, and what would have been. I was filled with thoughts about what should and should not happen, the what-ifs multiplied in my mind.

My friend Sonia would make powerful one-line statements; I called them Soniaism's. I'm sure if I told her the problem I had with worrying she would have given one her perfect Soniaism's.

One morning during my son's senior year of high school, he asked me if I wanted to take a walk after I came home from work. Surprised by his question, I said, "sure but what's the occasion?" He said, "I thought it would be nice to take advantage of this warm weather we've been having lately." I came home at about 4:00 PM and he was home awaiting my arrival. After five minutes into the walk, he said, "Mom, I know you have been worrying a lot and trying not to, so I thought coming on this walk may help you relax." He said, "do you remember what Ms. Ruth said at church? She said we have to have a "greater is He" mentality. No matter what you are worried about you have to trust God, who is bigger than us, to handle our situation. Mom, you are always talking to us about faith and the importance of faith. How is your faith holding on?" He continued, "I can still remember one of the three things you use to say to Sissy and me every morning before school. You would tell us that in everything we do, we have to make a choice. And with that choice there is a consequence. Then you would ask us for some examples of the choices we have to make. So now, mom, what choice are you going to make? Are you going to let worry take up your time and energy or exercise your faith?" He was right. I had become disconnected from my faith. Before this period of my life, I was connected to my faith, nothing was off-limits.

While he was talking I was praying in my spirit. I knew God was using him to help me and I thanked him for allowing God to use him in that way. When we got to the gate of our front yard, he stopped and said, "Mom, we just have to press towards the mark." He said, "You have the authority to confront your worry and tell the devil to get behind you." Right there we prayed.

What I have learned about making changes and progressing through life, one chapter to the next, is that I wouldn't be satisfied with where I was going until I was able to accept and appreciate the present. In order for change to take place and for me to start living the life I wanted, I had to start living for today. Letting go of my "should" has been one of the most powerful ways I changed my life.

Today things are very different. I have no more useless worrying, shame, regret, or getting caught in the should have, could have, would have stories about myself or other people. I have my morning routine which clears my heart and head before the day begins and allows me to start my day with peace of mind. I pray, I read, I exercise, I recite my money mantra, and recite my word of the year "self-discipline" that is written on my mirror with a dry erase marker.

Start your day with purpose and intentionality. Equally important, surround yourselves with people who are going in the same direction and who bring good energy your way. We have to trust that if we take action, results will follow. The biggest challenge often comes with getting out of our own way and allowing ourselves to take action.

CHAPTER 12

◆━❦━◆

Call To Action:
Building Your Identity

*"To live a remarkable life, you must take
consistent action in spite of your fears and
doubts." – Tony Fahkry*

I nterviews are scheduled and off to a great start. We have
narrowed the list down to the top three candidates. The first
two candidates were stellar, hitting every mark and each doing something to blow the Human Resource (HR) Manager away.
Candidate three is fifteen minutes late and the HR Manager tells
me to cross him off the list and to mark interviews officially
complete. As the HR Manager is standing at my desk the candidate arrives, thirty minutes after his scheduled interview, soaking
wet, and appearing to be out of breath. Before I could tell him
that the interviews are over, he explains that there was a car accident causing traffic to come to a complete stop. He describes
how he got out of the taxi and run here in the rain. The HR man-

ager immediately got him a cup of coffee and invited him into her office. As he sat down in her office she said, "You're hired, go home, put on dry clothes and I'll see you tomorrow morning at 9:00 am." He had an impressive resume and demonstrated dedication and commitment. He became the best of the best in our organization, surpassing his colleagues in leadership, training and team growth.

Candidate three was late and his appearance wasn't interview ready, but the HR manager listened to what he said and how he spoke and took that as her "call to action." She knew from that brief interaction he would be valuable to the team. He demonstrated passion and potential, and she took a chance on him. Has anyone ever taken a chance on you? Have you ever taken a chance on someone? Maybe it's time to make a call to action and take a chance on you.

In business, a call to action is a solicitation from the business owner that prompts a customer or potential customer to take a desired action. The same is true for making a call to action on living. You are the customer taking a chance on you, advocating for and recognizing your potential to create the life you want to live.

Part of renewing your authentic self is building your identity. You have to be intentional about taking a call to action to build or rebuild your identity. You must do so with an open mind, accepting who you are. This vulnerability is built on self-awareness, acceptance, trust, and faith of a call to action on our lives.

After going through that physically abusive relationship I was learning to take off a mask and start from where I was. I had to get out of my way and stop lying to myself and pretending that my life was perfect. Learning to renew my authenticity required me to be vulnerable, unguarded, and make a call to action in order to build my identity. A few things that I did:

- I began to share my story about what was going on with someone I worked with and respected on many levels. After sharing with Garlena what was happening, her immediate actions came as no surprise; she asked if the kids and I were safe, then she prayed, and pointed me in the direction to get help. She did not judge.

- I began to write about my experiences. I realized that while I didn't like what happened to me, I didn't want to forget it either. I didn't want to forget the kicks, the punches, the screaming, the bruises, the hurt, the pain, or the escape. I did not want to become complacent or make excuses for the things that transpired that night.

The more I wrote, the more comfortable I became with who I was. I no longer worried about the things that use to consume me and kept me from opening up:

- I didn't want to be seen as weak

- I didn't want to be judged

- I didn't want to be vulnerable

- I didn't want to be ostracized

When I made a call to action on myself, I took some time to get to know myself better. When making a call to action on ourselves we have an understanding of our own personality, values, belief system, character, goals, and purpose. You have to find out what you are good at and what things you love doing and understand when things about you and your personality change.

While growing up I was considered a friendly and respectful young lady. I was very social; I didn't struggle to make friends. I had friends from all the different sides of town, I even had friends that I met in elementary school who lived on the side of town where a young black girl dares not go alone. I didn't know it then, but I was an extrovert. I loved people. I was exposed to so many opportunities of meeting people and going different places that my social skills were developed early on, a lot of that had to do with the era I grew up in and the opportunities my mother took full advantage of. I attended summer camp every summer, I went to overnight camp for a 5-9-day period, I went with my godparents every other weekend, and I went to my father's baseball games. On occasion, we traveled to New York to visit family and friends. I played the violin, was a cheerleader for eight years and I on the drill team. I took cooking, sewing, and dance classes. I was in a youth leadership group and I was in a few pageants: Miss Crispus Attucks and Miss Fine Brown Frame; where I was selected as Miss Congeniality (that makes my kids laugh every time they hear that). All of these activities involved meeting and interacting with a lot of new people and I loved every minute of it.

That experience helped me adjust well in the Navy. I knew myself very well but after many years some things about me started to change, I began to notice these changes as I was making the call to action on myself. I was no longer an extrovert; I finally understood my alone time is the best time. I don't wake up to my cell phone, I only look at the phone after I've been up for at least an hour and I do not carry it around with me all the time.

In my days as an extrovert I would make time for everyone and say yes to every invitation received – stretching myself. Now I make time for all the things and people I choose, with intention. I am more selective in my "yeses" and my social circle gets smaller and smaller, which I love and appreciate because less has definitely proven to be more.

Spending time alone and reflecting daily helps me stay aware of any changes within me, understanding my personality, values, beliefs, character, goals, purpose and passion.

I believe it's important and rewarding if we invest the time getting to know ourselves. The first personality assessment I took was the Keirsey Bates Temperament Sorter (KTS), which is one I understood very well. As a Navy Leadership Facilitator, I taught students that came through the Leadership Courses for five years. The results of my first personality type was ESTJ (extrovert), three years later it was ISTJ (introvert). The KTS is closely associated with the Myers-Briggs Type Indicator (MBTI). I have only taken the MBTI twice. The results were the same and taken before my last KTS assessment. Another assessment tool is the DISC behavior assessment which centers on four different personality traits: Dominance (D), Influence (I), Steadiness (S), and Conscientiousness (C). It is a powerful do-it-yourself training and development tool that is designed to improve productivity, teamwork, and communication. I recommend the DISC for individuals and team assessments because of its simplicity: it's easy to understand and it works. For more information about the D.I.S.C. assessments go to www.inspiireleadership.com.

The clearer we are about our purpose, values, beliefs, character, goals, and personality/behavior, the happier and more effective we will be. Your purpose is what you are designed to do, the reason for your existence. Not to be confused with passion which is what motivates and gets you going. Passion is for you and purpose is for others. Beliefs are assumptions we hold true based on past experiences (ex: moral, spiritual, social, political). Values are things we strongly believe in (ex: family, freedom, equality, honesty). Our character is a combination of our personality, values, and beliefs. Goals produce results. They are realistic, require action and are usually short term.

We have to engage in personal work to rebuild and understand our identity. After we have a clear understanding of who we are and where we want to go, we can formulate a personal plan of action to renew our authenticity.

At the end of the day, it all boils down to knowing who you are and what you want. When you know that, you find peace within yourself.

PART IV:

Release Your Authenticity: Making The Transformation

CHAPTER 13

Being Enough

> "Make your life a masterpiece, imagine no limitations on what you can be, have or do. – Brian Tracy

I can recall an incident while serving as a Chief Petty Officer at one of my sea duty commands; there was a young female Sailor whom I had seen throughout the command but did not work directly with. One day I was headed to a meeting and she stopped to ask me if she could speak with me about a personal issue she wasn't comfortable talking with anyone else about. I can assume I was relatable to her, as a female, African American, and in a leadership position. After she assured me she was safe, we set up a time and location to meet. During the meeting she began to share her issues, cares, and concerns. I asked her a few questions that only she could answer. The purpose of my line of questioning was to get to the root cause, and we did. Growing up she wasn't very liked. She was rejected and people would talk about her behind her back.

She was bullied and as a result she became someone she didn't like. She became mean, resentful, and carried anger in her heart towards people she met. Never giving anyone a chance forced her to be alone most of the time. She was miserable and hated the way she was portrayed to others. The only thing she seemed to like was spending time alone, but that time was not being spent valuably; she constantly ridiculed and compared herself to others. I explained to her that she was not giving others or herself a chance. What we discovered was she had to figure out who she was and learn to love that person. She began taking off the mask of anger, the mask she thought was protecting her from rejection and hurt. She fostered a relationship with herself, getting to know, accept, and love her inner self. It was then that she started releasing the authenticity that was within and began making her transformation. She believed she was enough. She began controlling her narrative and being the person, she was born to be.

Throughout that tour and even today, we remain in contact. She began knowing and loving herself in a way that allowed her to let others get close to her. She has been a wonderful leader and mentor to those around her. You have to love and accept yourself, flaws and all. Do not let anyone make you ashamed of who you are and never trade your authenticity for the approval of others.

No one, not one of us is perfect. It's sometimes easier to blame people, circumstances or life for our unhappiness and missteps. But when we take full responsibility for our own happiness and actions, (that doesn't mean it's our fault that something bad or difficult has happened, it only means we have a choice over what we do with that experience) we take the power back over our lives. We give ourselves the opportunity and permission to live a happier and more fulfilled life. No one should remain stuck feeling unhappy or that they aren't enough. You are enough.

Being enough does not mean you are without flaw or that you are everything. It doesn't mean that you don't need help or that you don't need anyone or anything. It means you recognize how much you need help and when to ask for help. You understand that the sum of who you are is enough just as you are. There may be things you want more of, or things you want to be more of, like more connected, more intentional, more authentic, more honest, more spirit filled, more direct and more open. Wanting more of things is not about changing yourself, it's about being yourself and demonstrating your enough-ness. Wanting more things is not a contradiction of being enough, they are all expressions of your enough-ness.

When I was younger, kids would get teased about many different things, especially if anything on your person was considered "big" — you were a definite target: big head, big eyes, big teeth and in my case, big lips. Everyone would tell me how much I looked like my dad and that I had his lips and bowed legs. They called me "whopper chopper, whopper lips, and whopper 2", my older brother being whopper 1. I was sensitive to this name-calling that sometimes was so harsh that I began trying to hide my lips. I made a daily habit of holding in my lips, especially when I was in a new setting or in the company of someone I did not know. By the time I was in eleventh grade the size of my lips and the name-calling didn't seem to bother me, I outgrew that complex. That was until I attended a Navy 16-week technical training, usually called class "A" school, in San Diego, California. Similar to Basic Training, "A" school students came from all across the United States. A few people asked me what happened to my upper lip, or if my lip was swollen. With those questions, I reverted back to my younger days and the complex about my lips was constantly on my mind. After telling my brother Jody how I was feeling he quickly responded, we called you sorrow woman and whopper lips when you were a kid, you are not a kid and your lips are not going anywhere so stop listening to other people and learn to live with your lips just the way they are, they're your lips.

Oh, how things have changed. When I was a kid, I would respond to the teasing on an emotional level and I believed almost everything that was said about me or what was thrown at me. Things are definitely different now. What has changed? After speaking to my brother, if anyone says anything about my beautiful lips or anything else for that matter, I would allow it to sting at first but keep it moving. No matter what anyone says about me, I will not accept their words as my truth. I know that I am enough for me.

I am enough just the way that I am because it is who I am. I am far from perfect, but I am enough, and I feel that in my soul. Being enough is so satisfying to me. It's not about what I do, who I know or where I've been. I've never boasted or bragged about my credentials, certifications, or degrees. I am enough just as I am and the same applies to you.

You are enough! You do not have to work to prove yourself to anyone else. God uniquely designed you just the way you are.

CHAPTER 14

◆─❦◆❂◆❦─◆

Control Your Narrative

*"My mission in life is not merely to survive, but
to thrive; and to do so with some passion, some
compassion, some humor, and some style."*
— Maya Angelou

While recovering from a surgery in the earlier part of January, I was sitting in my living room flipping through television channels and decided to watch Oprah's Super Soul Sunday. I didn't catch the episode from the beginning, I missed about 15 minutes of the show. Oprah was asking various celebrities a question. The celebrities included phenomenal speakers, spiritual teachers, and thought leaders. The question she asked: "What is the most difficult decision you had to make to fulfill your destiny?" Because I caught this episode somewhere about halfway through, I'm not sure who I'd missed, but the responses I did hear were from Howard Schultz, John Gray, Geneen Roth, Tony Robinson, Dr. Shefali Tsabary, and Glennon Doyle. I remember writing the question down,

79

thinking how thought-provoking it was, a question that would be great to generate conversation on my blog or social media post. When she got to Glennon Doyle, however, my mind shifted; I began thinking about what God had been showing me for the past seven days.

I was recovering and healing from back surgery very nicely and I felt strong enough, physically and mentally, to start planning my business schedule for the year. During the first seven days, God had shown me words like story, book, author, over and over on social media, through personal growth readings, and podcasts. To make things clearer, He allowed the name of a phenomenal business woman, whom I didn't know, show up in my Instagram feed multiple times. Because she was also an author, I thought God was giving me a message for my daughter, saying it was time for her to write her book and tell her story. I was wrong. After speaking with my daughter and praying, that message was not for my daughter. It was while listening to Glennon Doyle, that God made it crystal clear that He was telling "me" it was time for me to write a book.

Doing so would be the hardest decision I had to make to fill my destiny. Writing a book was nothing like launching a business, it wasn't learning to say no. It was God purposed, yet, I struggled with the when and what, the two things I was totally incorrect about. When I would write a book and what the book was going to be about. I thought I had a few more years before I would author my first book and I thought it would be about God's calling reigning over my desires. What made this decision difficult was having to share the personal stories, who might I offend, what push back and backlash I might receive? It was at that moment my prayer was answered, I was no longer contemplating writing a book, it was at that moment I made the only decision I could make, and God sent me the confirmation to do so; and that phenomenal business woman I spoke of, later became my publisher.

"What is the most difficult decision I had to make to fulfill my destiny? It would be writing a book, sharing my story of unmasking. That answer came when I was the least prepared, so I wasn't sure of the possibility of completion, but I put my trust in God and followed Him every step of the way. It was a God-ordained moment, it was God's plan for me to stop on that channel, hear that question and get the answer with clarity about writing my book. He gave me the answer right then and there.

Another God ordained moment for me was April 1996, when I was stationed on board my first ship. I had a great working relationship with my chain of command, my peers, and my watch team. Our department was performing well, and our Captain said our teamwork was remarkably impressive and that it was the reason we operated so well underway and in port. I was promoted to Leading Petty Officer in my division, three months later. The entire division was qualified in all required workstations and additional areas. I was volunteering at a local school and I was on the Damage Control Training Team. The more I learned the more I excelled, and I kept learning.

With my team excelling and receiving accolades, I was feeling proud and accomplished. Then the shock of my life hit me. A home pregnancy test confirmed I was pregnant. I was still getting my cycle, but the changes in my body were evident to me and then the home pregnancy test confirmed it. I didn't know what I was going to do. This pregnancy was unexpected, and I was on birth control but none of that mattered. It did not matter that the ship was going to be decommissioned in 10 months. It didn't matter that the ship was not getting underway for 10 months. It didn't matter that I was ranked at the top of my peer group, none of that mattered. The policy was, that upon notification of pregnancy you had to leave the ship.

I could hear the response of others in my head; why would she get pregnant while on sea duty? What about the department? She just set her career back. All of those accolades I mentioned went right out the window, I felt like I let everyone down, and that I would be blackballed. I didn't know how to tell anyone at work, I didn't want to tell them, so I didn't.

What did I do next? I immediately donned the biggest mask of all time. The mask of secrecy and shame. I didn't know exactly how far along I was, but I was guessing about 2-3 months. The temperature in my workspace was always very cold, so I could get away with wearing my jacket at all times to help cover it up. I had duty every five days, which required that I stay overnight onboard the ship. I truly felt I was navigating uncharted territory but couldn't muster up the courage to share my truth. Home was the only place I could speak about my pregnancy. I spoke about it with my mom, my siblings, and my favorite cousin Veronica, but none of them knew I had not told anyone on the ship. This went on for about 3 months. Finally, I decided I was going to take some vacation days and when I got back, I would let my leadership team know about my condition.

I took two weeks off of work and while I was off I had a doctor's appointment. At that appointment, the doctor gave me the pregnancy notification to turn into my ship and he also made me an appointment with an OB/GYN.

That appointment was scheduled for the Monday I was due back at work. At that appointment the OB/GYN said I was 20 weeks;

I had been wearing the secrecy and shame mask for 20 weeks. I left that appointment with extreme leg pain, so extreme that I could barely drive, so I went to the emergency room. Everything that followed happened so fast it seemed like a whirlwind. When the emergency room doctor examined me, he said, the reason you are in so much pain is that you're having labor in your legs and your baby is trying to come. They admitted me into the hospital and 4 hours later my son was born, 7 weeks early, underweight but healthy, thank God. I was not 20 weeks pregnant; I was much further along.

I realized afterward how terrible of a decision hiding my pregnancy was. After the initial shock, the outpouring of love and support was overwhelming. While I was in the hospital I had to speak to the chaplain, social worker, and a therapist. If I hadn't let the anxiety, shame, and fear overtake me during my pregnancy, I could have enjoyed it so much more. I continuously thank God for keeping me and my son safe. I learned so many things during this period of my life. I now know that with Him, I am in control of my narrative. I control my actions, my words, my thoughts and I am intentional with the use of them all.

Years later I was still one of those leaders who thought getting help was a sign of weakness. Having those thoughts forced me to be strong and not show any signs of weakness. Many of my peers thought I was strong, that I could handle any situation without breaking a sweat. But I now realize that was just one of the repercussions of my smiling depression. I succeeded with my smiling mask. I projected an image of happiness and stability that no one knew what was really going on inside. They didn't know that my ability to cope with every little thing was a lie, and in reality I was just like everyone else – in need of help.

The ability to leave no hint that my world was secretly falling apart, while projecting constant happiness was a constant struggle for me. It often left me completely exhausted by the end of the day. When my mood decreased and my disappointments and frustrations increased, I was unable to cope with even the simplest of things; that is when I had my nightly breakdowns. After the kids had gone to bed and the house had quieted down, when I was alone with the lights down and the TV off: I would sit and cry.

There are things about who we are that are there to teach us, sometimes to show us a way to change or improve ourselves. Be careful, though, not everything about you needs to change, sometimes it's simply your perception of yourself that needs to change. Being authentic and totally honest with yourself can be uncomfortable but do it anyway and get comfortable being un-comfortable. Being brave enough to completely own all of who you are takes courage, but it's doable, so do it. The braver you become the easier it is to keep the mask off as you move forward and make decisions about your life that are aligned with your purpose and your truth.

Moving forward often requires the decision to cut ties with what-ever is holding us back, the physically seen and unseen. The word decision comes from the Latin word *decidere,* literally meaning to cut off. Are there things hindering you from reaching your goals? What, or who, do you need to cut off in order to move in the direction of your goals and dreams?

In the movie Rocky IV, there is an inspiring scene where Rocky teaches his son many life lessons in a short 3-minute period. One of those lessons was about placing the blame on others. He tells his son, "Somewhere along the line you changed, you stopped being you, you let people stick a finger in your face and tell you that you're no good. And when things got hard you went looking for something to blame like a big shadow." He later goes on to tell him, "Now if you know what you're worth, then go out and get your worth, but you gotta be willing to take the hits and not point fingers saying you ain't where you wanna be because of him or her or anybody."

Unfortunately, we often overlook our role and responsibility in our decision making or lack of goal accomplishment. That's why many people get stuck in victim mode. They blame their spouse, work, boss, circumstances, and anyone or anything else and skip right over taking responsibility for their own mess. The only one standing in your way or stopping you is you. Not your family, not your finances, not your education, not your friends, not the lack of opportunity. You are the only person standing in the way of accomplishing your goals, your dreams, your growth, and your greatness. Sadly, our limiting beliefs get in the way and as a result, we aren't aware of our self-sabotaging behaviors.

Letting down your guard and being totally vulnerable was extremely difficult for people like me. But when you have a desire to change and you truly look inside yourself for the nerve to do so, becoming the person you want to be is far less frightening. Even less so, when you control your narrative.

Allow yourself to release any guilt or self-limiting beliefs. Let the past stay in the past — it's over, behind you. Live in the present moment and be at peace with your identity. This process may be gradual, which okay. Breathe, be patient, and your real self will surface.

CHAPTER 15

―――◆◦✖◦◆―――

Check Your "Me Box"

> *"When we self-regulate well, we are better able to control the trajectory of our emotional lives and resulting actions based on our values and sense of purpose. – Amy Leigh Mercree*

One of the many things I enjoyed while in the Navy was chairing Career Development Boards. The Career Development Boards was a tool the Navy practiced to promote retention and maintain stable manpower. It provided the necessary guidance to newly reporting Sailors, so that they could make informed career decisions based on Navy policies, programs, and procedures. We would also use that time getting to know the Sailor better and I would end the session talking about the "Me Box". The "me box" focused on the three F's: family, finance, and fitness. I used the "me box" analogy to show Sailors the importance of taking care of themselves, their family, their health and their finances. I needed them to take care of those things so when they came to work, they would be fully present and able to focus on the mission of the command.

Like those Sailors, everyone needs to make time to take care of themselves first. No one can completely take care of you the way that you can. I'm not talking about the occasional manicure, pedicure, massage, or soaking in a hot tub. Checking your "me box" (some call this self-care) is something that is done daily.

Once upon a time, there was a cobbler who lived in a large village and was the only cobbler in town. He was responsible for repairing the boots of everybody else and was always very busy.

So busy in fact that he didn't have time to repair his own boots. Initially, that wasn't a problem, but over time, his boots began to deteriorate and fall apart. While he worked busily on the boots for everyone else, his feet became blistered and he started to walk with a limp. His customers started to worry about him, but he reassured them that everything was okay. However, after a few years, the cobbler's feet were so injured that he could no longer work, and no one's boots were repaired. As a consequence, the entire town started to limp in pain, all because the cobbler never took the time to repair his own boots.

Darren Poke wrote this story to illustrate a simple principle that is so often disregarded.

"If you don't look after yourself, after a while you'll be no good to anyone else. Your best intentions will mean nothing, and you'll be unable to do what you're meant to do."

Think about the safety procedures onboard an airplane, demonstrated by the flight attendant or a video prior to takeoff. The warning to travelers is clear, "in case of emergency, you must first put on your own oxygen mask before helping anyone." They tell you this because when you save yourself first you have a better chance of saving anyone that may be traveling with you. Otherwise, if you try to put someone else's mask on first, you are susceptible of passing out before you can completely help them get their mask on.

We can't take care of our families, careers, hobbies or anything of importance if we don't first take care of ourselves; mind, body, and soul. Make it your daily habit to take care of yourself. God has given us one life and one chance to live it so live it well.

My husband has always gone to bed at a decent time on the weekdays. It had to be something really important for him to stay up past 10:00 pm. He and the kids were on good schedules and got plenty of rest. I, on the other hand, would be up long after they all went to sleep. Sometimes I would go to sleep and wake up after only getting a few hours of sleep because my mind would be racing. Sleep was not a priority for me, nor did I value its importance. All of that changed when I attended a sleep hygiene class once a week for four weeks. What a huge eye-opener! As a result of taking that class, I established a regular bedtime hour or time frame, stopped drinking caffeine, and added a few other things to my schedule. Getting a healthy amount of sleep on a regular basis is critical to my total health and wellness.

As I was growing in my authenticity and in alignment with my purpose, it gave me the fuel I needed to live a happier and more productive life. I realized the importance of taking care of my spiritual, physical, and mental health and realized the importance it had on my mind, body, and soul. Here are a few of my favorite things that give me the greatest self-satisfaction. These things have had a direct impact on maintaining balance and played a significant part in my overall health.

Spiritually. Things I love to do for my spiritual health are; listening to worship and soaking music, attending church and bible study, and sitting in the quiet. Every day I recite my morning mantra out loud "Good morning Lord. I love you Lord. Thank you Lord for waking me up today." And special thanks to my sister, soror, and dear friend Labrisha I've added, "I trust this day to you, Lord."

Physically. For my body, I focus on three primary areas; proper nutrition, physical activity, and sleep hygiene (eat, sleep, and exercise).

- I have not eaten red meat since 2016 and I have not eaten meat or anything that has a mother since 2017. I enjoy eating and pre-paring nutritional meals. Meal prepping, trying new recipes, and exchanging recipes with my friend Kelly have become a small hobby for me. I still love snacks, especially potato chips from my hometown and I treat myself to them whenever I get the chance.

- Sleep and rest have moved significantly up on my list of priorities.

- Cycling, walking, yoga, swimming, and racquetball are at the top on my list. I find yoga and walking the most relaxing and I'm also able to clear my mind at the same time. Even when I have restrictions exercise is still a priority. With limitations walking has become my go to activity.

We should approach caring for our physical body holistically be-cause it undeniably functions as one. You cannot do exercise on your legs without impacting your back nor can you say that your back pain has no impact on the rest of your body; of course it does, everything we do to one part affects the whole body.

Mentally. For the mind I love to practice mindfulness and grati-tude journaling, they both strengthen my brain. My mental health affects how I think, feel, and act, so I pay particular attention to the company that I keep. Staying positive keeps my mood from being dragged down and I try to avoid conversations involving negative talk. I find that helping others satisfies my soul and try to do so whenever I am able. I also have truth rants. Truth rants are speaking affirmations aloud and into the universe. Some examples would be: The truth is I am brave, I am capable, I am strong and if I fall, I will get back up because I am a winner. The truth is perfectionism does not exist. The truth is no one and nothing defines my worth. The truth is I define my worth. The truth is rejection means nothing. The truth is I can mess things up and try again. The truth is I love m. and I am enough. The truth is I don't care if someone doesn't like me, it doesn't mean I don't live out my purpose.

For me taking care of the physical, spiritual and mental all work together and go hand-in-hand. When I eat well, I get good rest. When I take care of my spirit, my mental wellness stays in balance. Being preventive and following healthy routines can help you deal with stress, help with your mental function, improve your self-esteem and help face challenges down the road.

We have to fully embrace wellness to improve the mind, body, and soul. When you make spiritual, physical, and mental wellness a priority, you maximize your potential to live a productive life and your overall health improves.

The way you end your day is equally important as the way you start your day. Here is a list of my Life Focused Habits that consistently create positive energy, improve performance and better

results. In addition to praying, five of these things which are bolded, I do every night before I go to bed. I reflect, read, write, express gratitude, and pray. I don't do them all at the same time

or in any specific order, I just like to make sure I do each one of them before I go to sleep.

- I reflect daily.

- I always act with a purpose.

- I pray, read and laugh often.

- I journal and gratitude daily.

- I take responsibility for my results.

- I don't wait for perfection; instead, I act now.

- I learn more from my failures than my successes.

- I spend time alone with God and with the people I love.

- I use both negative and positive feedback to stay on target.

- I take my work seriously, but I do not take myself too seriously.

- I am intentional about my spiritual, physical, and mental health.

Start your day with purpose and give a little attention to yourself, even if only 10 minutes. If you can make it 30 minutes, great. It doesn't matter how little you start with, it's just important that you start.

CHAPTER 16

Be the Person
You Were Born to Be

> "I believe there's a calling for all of us. I know
> that every human being has value and purpose.
> The real work of our lives is to become aware.
> And awakened. To answer the call." – Oprah
> Winfrey

When my son was a baby, my daughter, who was two years older, and I would play with him all the time. While we played with him, I would say to him "hey little man, hey little man." I said it so much that his sister started calling him "Man-Man." The name stuck and everyone else started doing the same. When he began learning how to talk he couldn't pronounce his sister's name, so he just started calling her "Sissy." Fast forward six years later we were at the park and his sister called him to come over to the merry-go-round where she was playing. When he came over to the merry-go-round, he calmly said to her, "don't call me Man-Man anymore call me by my real name." We were both shocked by what he said but she said "okay" and they continued playing. Later that night when he was getting ready to get into the bed I asked him, "why don't you want to be called Man-Man any longer?" He said, "I want people to call me by my real name, the name I was born with, not my nickname" and that was the day we stopped calling him Man-Man. However, as of today he still calls his sister "Sissy."

Everyone is different. We each have our unique purpose and we were all born with our individual inherent talent, skills, and passions. Sometimes we get so caught up with competing requirements of the everyday hustle and bustle that we don't think much about being who we were born to be.

For me, my mistakes led me to find out first who I wasn't. When I truly learned I was not any of the masks I wore, metaphorically, I sent all those masks down the garbage disposal to be chopped into shreds, never to be recycled again. After the destruction comes the work. You can't think your way into becoming who you were born to be, you have to get on the grind and do the work to release your authenticity and make the transformation to be who you were born to be.

I choose to:

- Trust God completely.

- Treat mankind fairly.

- Really live.

- Not be afraid of anything

- Walk boldly towards life.

- Believe I can achieve anything.

- Be myself, with pride.

- Be guided by my morals, always.

- Speak my mind, because it's my truth.

- Enjoy and savor life with my family.

After acknowledging the mask, you are wearing, begin living authentically. Look at yourself in the mirror, you will begin to find that sweet spot and drop your mask. Start from where you are and get out of your own way. Understand that you are enough and check your "me box." You are ready to be the person you were born to be. When you do these things, with your eyes wide open, you are prepared to live in ways that are aligned with your deepest beliefs, values, dreams, and desires. Being authentic is far more important than appearing to be perfect.

Whenever I went through a rough patch in my life, the three things that remained with me were my faith, my hope, and love. Those are the three things that can't be taken from me. They are the only things we really need.

The moment you start being yourself all the time and not part time, you'll reveal your authentic self and share your uniqueness and glorious gifts with the rest of the world.

So, take off your mask. Lay down your shame. Let go of fear. Never be afraid to show your true self. You are a child of God with nothing to be ashamed of. Let your light shine! Be who you were born to be!

Individual Or Group
Discussion Questions

Questions to ask yourself that will help assess your authenticity. I find them to be insightful and enlightening:

1. *Who are the people or person that knows you best? How do you show up in their presence? How do you feel around them?*

2. *How are you most frequently misperceived and why? Who is the real you and why is it that others don't see that as much as you'd like them to?*

3. *What is the biggest masquerade in your life today? When do you feel the biggest disconnect between who you are and what you do? What were/are the circumstances that led you into this situation? How do you cope with or compensate for this feeling of disconnection? How do you think it affects the people and relationships in your life?*

4. *Do you admit when you make a mistake? Do you admit your mistake without the proverbial "but"? Without judging or blaming others?*

5. *If an objective observer watched you for 24 hours a day over the next 30 days, what do you think they would say are your three greatest strengths and your three greatest weaknesses? How do you feel about each of those six qualities?*

6. *Are you living your purpose? Is your life aligned with your values? Is your life aligned with your beliefs?*

My challenge to you: Set aside 30 minutes over the next five days to answer these questions. What do you notice about your responses? What surprises you? Leave a comment to share your thoughts at http://www.inspiireleadership.com

www.ingramcontent.com/pod-product-compliance
Lightning Source LLC
Chambersburg PA
CBHW021150090426
42740CB00008B/1024